Basic IT A

TRAI

GW01112485

Basic IT Assignments

Barry Mc Gettigan

Gill & Macmillan

Gill & Macmillan Ltd
Goldenbridge
Dublin 8
with associated companies throughout the world
© Barry Mc Gettigan 1998
0 7171 2656 0
Print origination in Ireland by Graham Thew Design

The paper used in this book is made from the wood pulp of managed forests. For every tree felled, at least one tree is planted, thereby renewing natural resources.

All rights reserved.
No part of this publication may be reproduced, copied or transmitted in any form or by any means without written permission of the publishers or else under the terms of any licence permitting limited copying issued by the Irish Copyright Licensing Agency, The Writers' Centre, Parnell Square, Dublin 1.

www.gillmacmillan.ie

For my parents

CONTENTS

Acknowledgments	vii
Part I The Basics	**1**
What is a Computer?	1
How Useful Are They?	1
The Computer Dissected	2
The Keyboard	4
Part II Word Processing	**6**
Basic Word Processing	6
Enhancements	8
Working with Blocks	11
Written Test	12
Justification	13
Business Letters	15
Proofreading and Spelling Checks	18
Page Set-Up	20
Find and Replace	21
Tabulation	23
Curriculum Vitae	26
Proofreading Symbols	28
Speed Tests	31
Fun with Word Proccessing	33
Questionnaire	34
Valentine's Day Card	35
Invitation	36
Newsletter	37
Assessment Log Book	39
Part III Databases	**40**
What is a Database?	40
Where are Databases Used?	40
Fields and Records	41
Field Width	41
Field Datatype	42
Searching Records	45
Sorting Records	49
Adding/Deleting Fields	55
Written Test	56
Using Maths on Fields	57
More about Sorts	61
Enhancements	66
Indexing	68
Assessment Log Book	78

Part IV Spreadsheets	**79**
Introduction	79
Screen Layout	80
Cell Address	80
Cell Attributes	80
Enhancements	83
Sum and Range	86
Copying Formulae	89
Average, Maximum and Minimum	92
Absolute Cell Address	96
Adding/Deleting Rows and Columns	100
Written Test	102
Charts and Graphs	103
Using 'IF'	110
Assessment Log Book	117
Combined Assignment	**118**
Part V The Internet	**122**
Introduction	122
Parts of the Net	123
Creating a Site	125
Sites of Interest	126

ACKNOWLEDGMENTS

I would like to thank my family and friends and all those who have helped me with this book. Thanks to Hubert Mahony in Gill & Macmillan for his advice. A special thank you to my wife Dymphna for her tireless support and encouragement.

SOLUTIONS

Solutions to assignments in this book are available on the internet at
www.gillmacmillan.ie/basicitsolutions
from September 1998

PART I THE BASICS

What is a Computer?

Computers have been around for quite a while now—in fact, the abacus is considered to be the first computer ever constructed. Most of us learned basic addition and subtraction using this computer. A slide rule is another example of a computer. To compute means to calculate or to figure out.

Some History

The first modern computers were mechanical adding machines invented by Charles Babbage (1792–1871). The first of these was the Difference Engine. Although designed in the 1820s, it was only built in 1991. This machine is composed of cogs and wheels which are set and turned by hand. It is currently on view in the Science Museum in London.

Some Changes

Computers have gone through a series of important changes since the electric computers of the 1940s. At that time they were huge devices, as big as a four-storey building, and cost millions of pounds to build. They were temperamental and often broke down. This was because the vacuum tubes inside them, which were responsible for relaying information, often exploded and had to be replaced. Lots of people were required just to replace the broken tubes!

The next big step came with the introduction of the transistor, which was developed in 1948 by Bell Telephone Laboratories. **Transistors** replaced the troublesome vacuum tube. As a result, the size of computers decreased dramatically and their performance improved. Fewer staff were required to operate them and the cost decreased (although they were still too expensive for most businesses).

Computers Today

The invention of integrated circuits heralded a new era in computing. Nowadays, all the transistors in a computer are held on a single slice or wafer of silicon. This is what we call the **silicon chip**. Today's computers are compact, very powerful and reliable.

How Useful Are They?

Computers are used in many different places and situations: in schools, banks, government offices, supermarkets, NASA, film studios, etc. They perform a wide variety of functions and tasks. These can range from computer animations and the control of spacecraft, to reading the barcode on a tin of beans. They help us to work with words (word processing), to work with numbers (spreadsheets), and to sort and search information (databases). They can also be used to prepare plans for houses and buildings (computer-aided design or CAD).

What Will I Learn?

We are going to look at word processing, databases and spreadsheets—the three most common types of computer application. Many computers come with these applications already installed. But before we do that, let's look at the different parts of the computer and see what each part does.

The Computer Dissected

A computer can be divided in to four main parts: **input devices**, **the processor**, **storage** and **output devices**.

Input Devices Input devices allow us to interact with the computer. In other words, we give information to the computer through the input devices. There are lots of different ways of doing this and the most common ways are listed below.

INPUT DEVICE	DESCRIPTION
KEYBOARD	Keys are pressed and characters appear on the screen. Irish keyboards are called QWERTY because these are the first six letters on the top row.
MOUSE	A small hand-held device with a ball inside. Moving the mouse causes an arrow to appear on the screen. Clicking the mouse makes a selection.
SCANNER	A laser reads the lines on a barcode and translates this information in to product information, e.g., name, price, stock number, etc.
TOUCHSCREEN	Touching the screen allows choices to be made. Often found in cinemas and information booths in national parks.
OPTICAL MARK RECOGNITION	A scanner reads a mark. Used in LOTTO machines and to evaluate some aptitude tests.
OPTICAL CHARACTER RECOGNITION	A scanner reads text. Used for the payment of bills.
VOICE	Speaking to the computer allows the user to issue commands, write text, etc.
MAGNETIC CARD READER	Used in ATMs and to read tickets on buses.

The Processor This is the 'brain' of the computer. The processor contains millions of tiny transistors, all of which fit on to a silicon chip. This chip is no bigger than a postage stamp! The processor is divided in to different areas which control calculations and programmes. Some processors are given numbers as names, e.g., 286, 386 and 486. The bigger the number, the faster and more complex the processor. Others have proper names, such as the Pentium chip. It all depends on the chip manufacturer. Another important part of the processor is *memory*.

A computer's memory is divided in to two main parts: ROM and RAM. Let's look at ROM first.

ROM ROM means Read Only Memory. It stores all the instructions that the computer needs to function. It is permanent and cannot be changed. It is easy to visualise its role if you think of a book—you can read a book many times but you can't change the story. The story stays the same no matter how many people read it.

RAM

The second type of memory in a computer is called RAM. This stands for Random Access Memory (not a male sheep!). A computer's RAM is the working space in which you create and modify documents. It's where the computer stores information while you're working on it. The information stored in RAM is stored there temporarily and is lost once the computer is switched off. That is why you should always save your work before you finish up.

Storage

Because RAM is temporary and ROM cannot be changed, you must have a place to save your work. Sometimes this can be the hard disk inside your computer or, more often, you will save your files to a floppy disk.

Output Devices

Output devices allow the computer to show us what it has just done. There are two main output devices: the monitor and the printer.

The Monitor

The monitor, or visual display unit (VDU), shows the user information on a screen. There are many different types of monitor (don't call them TVs!) and the quality of the picture depends on the number of dots (pixels) on the screen. The more pixels the better the image.

The Printer

Printers allow us to print from the computer. There are two main types: IMPACT printers and NON-IMPACT printers. Impact printers print by hitting pins on an inked ribbon. They are often called dot-matrix printers. They are very noisy and can't print graphics. Non-impact printers produce a much better quality printout and can often print in colour. Ink-jet and laser printers are non-impact printers. You may have seen these advertised with the letters DPI. This stands for Dots Per Inch. The more dpi a printer can produce, the better the quality of the printout.

The four parts of the computer described above are known as the FOUR-STAGE MODEL. They form the computer HARDWARE, that is, the physical part of the computer. SOFTWARE is the part you cannot touch, such as the programmes and applications.

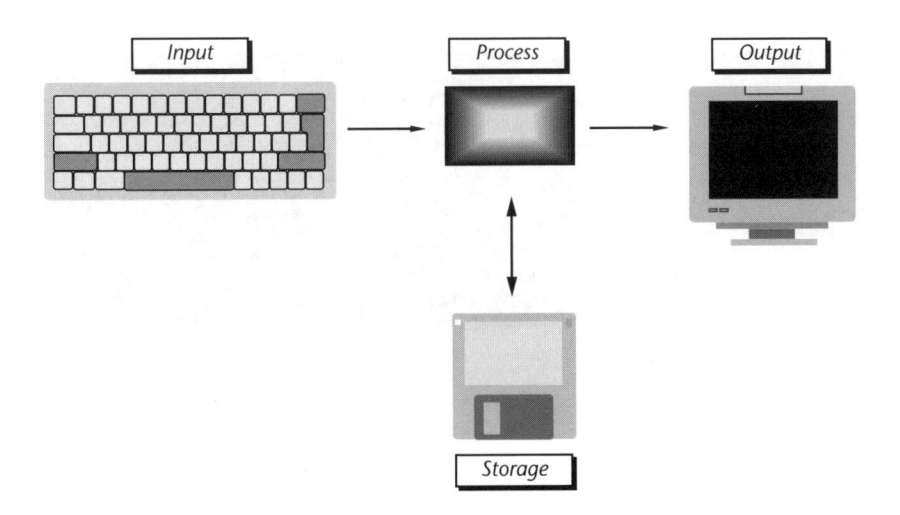

Input → Process → Output

Storage

The Keyboard

Keyboarding is like skateboarding—the more you practise, the better you get. The keyboard is one of the most common ways of inputting text and numbers in to a computer. We will now look at the keyboard to familiarise ourselves with it. Try to locate the following keys: SHIFT, ENTER, BACKSPACE, SPACEBAR.

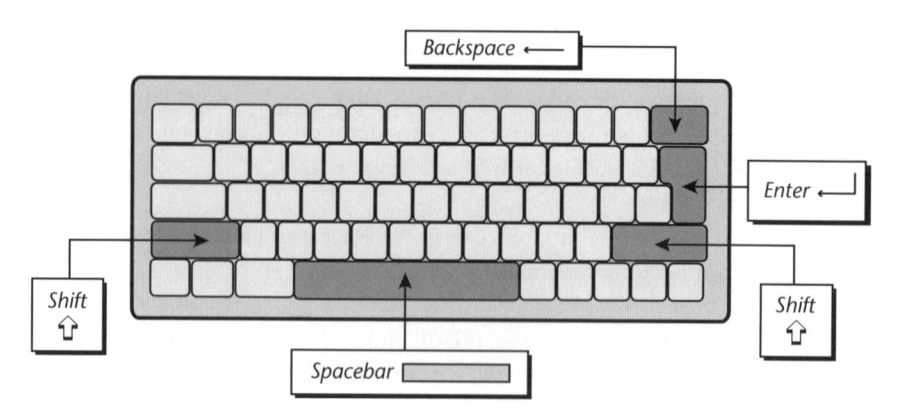

What Do These Keys Do?

The SHIFT key is used to make CAPITAL LETTERS and also to select the second character on a key. For example, if you hold down the SHIFT key and press the number 5 on your keyboard, then '%' will appear on your screen.

The RETURN or ENTER key is used to make a new paragraph in most word processing programmes. It is also used to indicate that a command should proceed.

The BACKSPACE key is used to delete characters to the left of the cursor.

The SPACEBAR is used to make a space between words.

Frequently Made Mistakes (Oops!)

No space after a comma or period (full stop).

Too many spaces after a comma or period—there should only be one space after either of these.

All the letters are in capitals—most probably because the CAPS LOCK button is on.

If your word processor has word wrapping capabilities, never press ENTER to go on to a new line. Your word processor will automatically move words on to a new line. This is called 'word wrap'.

Assignment no. 1

In your first assignment we will look at the different ways of keying in text and numbers. Type everything below exactly as you see it. Use CAPS LOCK when typing a long list of capitals, but don't forget to turn it off for normal typing! Use the SHIFT key when typing one or two capitals and to type the pound sign (above 3) and exclamation mark (above 1).

> BIG BIG BARGAINS IN THE BARGAIN SHOP
> There are hundreds of bargains this weekend in the BARGAIN SHOP. Just look at the prices below. HUGE SAVINGS!
> CLOTHING
> ARAN SWEATERS Were £30.00 NOW £15
> CORDUROYS Were £25.00 NOW ONLY £15
> SHIRTS Were £15 NOW AN AMAZING £5
> This offer MUST END SOON!

Assignment no. 2

> This is my second assignment. I am gradually getting to know the keyboard but sometimes I can get stuck looking for keys. For example, the comma key, the & sign, the % sign and the full stop.
>
> The difference between a colon (:) and a semi-colon (;) is small but very important.
>
> I realise that accuracy is vital to keyboarding.
>
> Signed
>
> Your name

How did you do? Practice makes perfect in keyboarding. It is important to be very careful when typing your work. Shoddy work leaves a very poor impression on the reader. Always check your spelling and punctuation (commas, periods, etc.). We are now going to turn our attention to *word processing*.

PART II WORD PROCESSING

Basic Word Processing

Word processing uses the power of the computer to rapidly format (change) text and documents. For example, we can easily type in some text, change its size and change the style (font). If we make mistakes we can easily correct them, or better still, get the computer to do it for us!

ADVANTAGES	DISADVANTAGES
easy to use	must have elementary skills
can save documents	cost of training and cost of machine
quality is very good	monitor can cause eye strain

Where is Word Processing Used?

Word processing is a widely used application. It is commonly used to produce DOCUMENTS, REPORTS, LETTERS, CONTRACTS and MAILSHOTS (a mailshot is advertising that is sent to a list of people and is sometimes called 'junk mail'). Can you think of any other uses?

Assignment no. 3

Find out the name of your word processing package and how to open it on the computer. Type in the text below and save your document as CARS. Your teacher will show you how to do this.

CARS

The car has been in existence for more than 80 years now. When the first prototypes were built, people were afraid of them—they called them 'horseless carriages'. Until then, of course, people travelled in a horse and carriage.

The first cars couldn't travel very fast either. In fact they were so slow someone would have to walk in front of the car waving a red flag. They were only allowed to travel at 4 m.p.h. in the country and 2 m.p.h. in towns!

In 1908, Henry Ford produced the first mass-produced car, the Model T. Around 15 million of these were made. Ford said that the car could be any colour as long as it was black!

Over the years cars have become more efficient and economical. They have also become faster and, as a result, accidents occur more frequently. Cars have come a long way from the first Model T.

When you are finished, check your spelling and punctuation.

Assignment no. 4

Now it's time to make some changes to your CARS document. Before you do that, however, you have to get the document back. This is called retrieving your file. Your teacher will tell you how to do this.

Beware! Many students make the mistake of saving a blank screen over their original document, wiping out all their work as a result.

To make a change, simply click your mouse on the word you want to change (or bring the cursor to the word with the arrow keys) and retype. To ADD words, just click where you want to add the words and type. To DELETE words, click and place the cursor where you want to delete. Then press the BACK-SPACE key (this will delete to the left of the cursor) or the DELETE key (this will delete to the right of the cursor).
Now make the following changes to your CARS document.

1. Insert 'or automobile' after 'The car' on line one, paragraph one.
2. Change '80' to 'eighty' on line one, paragraph one.
3. Remove the full stop after 'red flag' and insert 'to warn people of the oncoming danger!' on line two, paragraph two.
4. Change 'Henry Ford produced' to 'Henry Ford developed' on line one, paragraph three.

Save your work and check for spelling mistakes. Check also for spacing errors—remember, only one space after a comma or a full stop. When you are fully satisfied with your work, save it again.

Assignment no. 5

Type the text shown below and save the document as WATER.

Water is made up of two elements: hydrogen and oxygen. It contains twice as many hydrogen atoms as oxygen atoms.
As we know, water is a colourless, tasteless liquid which is vital for life. The human body is made up of 90% water.
The moon exerts a powerful influence on the water of the earth. This is reflected in the tides. The word 'lunatic' refers to the moon so perhaps it exerts an even more powerful influence than we know!

Now make the following changes.
1. Insert 'This is why it's called H2O.' at the end of the first paragraph.
2. In the second paragraph, insert '(if it's pure)' after 'tasteless'.
3. Delete 'made up of' in the second paragraph.

Check your spelling and save your work again.

Enhancements

Now you know how to create a document, how to save it, how to retrieve it and how to make changes to it. Next we will look at improving a document's appearance. This is called *enhancement* or *formatting*.

First, there are three new terms you need to know: bold, italic and underline.

BOLD	makes text **thick**
ITALIC	*slanting* text
UNDERLINE	underlining text

Your teacher will show you how to do this on your word processor. When you are ready, try the following assignments. Save your documents as ADS and PI respectively. Pretend that you are sending these advertisements to a free ads paper. Check your spelling!

Handy Hint: Type everything in, save it and then enhance the text. In this way, if you make a mistake it is easy to return to the original document.

Assignment no. 6

FOR SALE
COMPUTER Pentium 200 with *MMX* technology, 32MB RAM, graphics accelerator, 2GB hard drive, 16-speed CD-ROM, fax/modem. *Loads* of software, some still prepackaged. Unwanted prize. First £1200 secures. Telephone 09-123456 for further details.

CAR 1990 Peugeot 205 XRAD. Power Steering, Sunroof, *Electric Windows*, all leather interior. 50,000 genuine miles. Central locking. One owner from new. Taxed until end of August. Genuine reason for selling. Only £1500 or nearest offer. Reply to Box 1250.

Assignment no. 7

PRIVATE EYE
Perhaps you need my help. I am a private investigator and have many years' experience behind me. **All** my clients are important to me. No case is too small. Just read what some of my clients have said.

'Thank you Private Eye. You have saved my company over £2.5 *million* in lost revenue. If it hadn't been for your brilliant detective work, we would have lost the company.'

'Thank you for the return of Fluffy. We were sure he was dead.'

For further *confidential* information on the services of Private Eye, please post a stamped addressed envelope to the address below. Before it is too late.

Now let's look at two more ways of enhancing our document. The first is by changing the font and the second is by changing the size of the text.

Font is the style of type that you use. Here are a few different fonts: *Font*

this is Times New Roman
`this is Courier`
this is Gill Sans Condensed

Text can vary in size from very, **very big**, to very, very small. Size is measured in points. Size 10 is normal. This is the size you're looking at right now.   *Size*

Find out how to change the font and the size of the text on your word processor. Then try the following assignments. Remember, it's easier to change text after it has been typed and saved. Use size 16 for the heading and size 10 for the rest of the text. Save your documents as LIGHT and WOOD respectively.

Assignment no. 8

To Show that Light Travels in Straight Lines

1. Put a hole in the centre of three cards and place them in a straight line. Make sure they are aligned correctly by putting a thread through each card and pulling tightly.

2. Shine a light through the cards. The light is visible through the holes. If a card is moved, the light is no longer visible.

CONCLUSION: Light travels in straight lines.

Assignment no. 9

THE WOODWORK SHOP

We stock all types of tools for the woodworker.

SAWS
Hand saws, back saws, rip saws, panel saws, tenon saws, dovetail saws and coping saws.

PLANES
Jack planes, try planes, fore planes, block planes, rebate planes, router planes and spoke shaves.

HAMMERS
Claw hammers, pin hammers, cross-pein and a wide range of mallets.

AND MUCH MUCH MORE!

Assignment no. 10 In this assignment we are going to create a new document, save it and then enhance it. Type everything exactly as you see it and save your document as TV.

Now enhance your document by changing the font and the size of the text. Remember, don't go overboard! Two or three fonts is more than enough in a document.

> TELEVISION PROGRAMMES
>
> Television, the '*box in the corner*', plays a very big part in our lives. It can have a variety of influences on us, some good and some bad. It plays an important role in the education of our young. There are many examples of educational television, from David Attenborough's '*Life on Earth*' to '*Blackboard Jungle*'.
>
> However, TV also has another more destructive side. This is clearly evident in the amount of violence which is broadcast, often at times not suitable for family viewing (i.e., before 9.00 p.m.). This can lead to young people believing that this level of violence is justifiable and indeed the norm.
>
> Therefore, broadcasters and parents, those who control what we watch, have a grave responsibility. We should be entertained and educated by TV but it should not lead us to do things that are harmful, either to ourselves or to society in general.

Assignment no. 11 Type in the following assignment and enhance it as you see fit. Change the size of the headings, use bold, italic and underline, and change the fonts. Save the document as LIFE.

> ROCK-POOLS
>
> A walk along the sea-shore may seem the ideal way to relax after a week of school. But how many people ever look down at their feet or in to the rock-pools? The whole sea is teeming with life, from the largest whales to the smallest plankton.
>
> Every little rock-pool contains life. Some of this is visible to the naked eye, for example, small fish, seaweed and pondskaters, which run rapidly across the surface of the water. Most of the life in a rock-pool, however, is invisible and can only be viewed under a microscope. Diatoms, for example, have the most beautiful shells in the world despite their size!
>
> COLLECTION
>
> One of the simplest methods of collecting rock-pool life is to use a plankton net. You can make your own using a sheet of muslin. The plankton net will trap many of the smaller animals which you can then put into a jar and study at your leisure using a magnifying glass or microscope.

Working with Blocks

A *block* is a highlighted piece of text or data. Normally you can highlight or select text by placing your mouse at the beginning of the text, holding the left mouse button down, and dragging the mouse to the end of the text. The selected text will appear white against a black background. This selected text is called a block. If you do not have a mouse, ask your teacher how to do this.

What Can I Do With Blocks?

By blocking text you can rapidly format all the text in that block. Whatever you do only affects the selected text. Thus, you can easily change the look of an entire paragraph. You can also use blocks to CUT, COPY and PASTE sections of your text.

Cut

To CUT a block or selection of text means to remove it from where it is and keep a copy of it in memory. CUT is usually used with PASTE.

Copy

To COPY text means that the original selection stays where it is, but you keep a copy of it in memory. Again, this copied text is normally pasted somewhere else.

Paste

To PASTE a selection means to take a cut or copied block of text from memory and place it where the cursor is.

The terms CUT, COPY and PASTE are old expressions used in the printing industry. A copy of text would by cut (using scissors) from its position, gummed at the back and pasted in to a new position on the page.

Assignment no. 12

Now try the following assignment. Type in everything exactly as you see it and carry out the instructions below.

> To CUT a block or selection of text means to remove it from where it is and keep a copy of it in memory. CUT is usually used with PASTE.
>
> To COPY text means that the original selection stays where it is, but you keep a copy of it in memory. Again, this copied text is normally pasted somewhere else.
>
> To PASTE a selection means to take a cut or copied block of text from memory and place it where the cursor is.

For You To Do

1. Select the first paragraph and CUT it out.
2. PASTE the first paragraph after the last paragraph.
3. Select the second paragraph and COPY it.
4. Insert the copy of the second paragraph after the last paragraph using the PASTE command.
5. If you have time, try selecting a paragraph of text and changing its size and font.

Written Test

These questions are designed to test how well you understand all the concepts explained so far. Good luck!

1. Name the four main parts of the computer (the four-stage model).

2. Name any four input devices and give a brief description of each.

3. Distinguish between hardware and software.

4. What are the advantages and disadvantages of word processing?

5. For which of the following would you use a word processor?

A. Letters C. Contracts

B. Drawings/graphics D. Making postcards

6. Why do you have to save a document?

7. What is a font?

Hand out

8. [illegible]

9. What [illegible]

10. Explain how you would [illegible] paragraph of text.

Justification

11. Which of the following [illegible]

A. this **text** C. this text

B. this text D. this text

12. What are the differences between ROM and RAM?

13. Pressing ENTER every time you want to go on to the next line is OK. True or false?

14. How would you CUT a section of text?

15. Explain the difference between CUT, COPY and PASTE.

Justification

Justification refers to the way text is arranged on the screen or page.

Text is normally LEFT justified. This means that the left-hand side of the text is straight, like this paragraph.

Left

This paragraph is centred or CENTRE justified. That means that all the text on a line is an equal distance from the sides of the page.

Centred

This line is RIGHT justified. That means that the text lines up against the right-hand side.

Right

The final type of justification is called FULL, or sometimes it is simply referred to as JUSTIFIED. It looks like columns of text in a newspaper. Both the left- and right-hand sides are straight.

Full

Type the text below using the different justifications as shown.

Assignment no. 13

For You To Do

> Justification refers to the different ways text is aligned on a page or screen. Most text is left justified, i.e., the text has a straight left edge. This is the most widely used form of justification. It is easy on the eye and looks neat when printed on a page.
>
> Some text can be centred. This is common in menus where each line is centred.
> Take the following example:
> Egg Mayonnaise
> Smoked Salmon on Brown Bread
>
> Text can also be right justified. This often occurs in addresses. Take the following example:
> John McEntee
> 121 Mount Eagle Street
> Kilkenny
>
> This text is fully justified. That means that the computer will add or subtract spaces within the text to make it straight on both the left- and right-hand sides. This is often used in newspapers and sometimes in novels.

1. CUT the first paragraph and insert it after the centred text.
2. COPY the centred text and insert another copy after the last paragraph.
3. Make the last paragraph RIGHT justified instead of fully justified.
4. Save the document as JUSTIFY.

Assignment no. 14 You have landed a summer job in your local hotel. The manageress has asked you to create a dinner menu. She wants the menu to be easy to read and attractive. Finally, she gives you the details to be included in the menu.

For You To Do

STARTER

Egg Mayonnaise
Summer Salad
Oysters
Prawn Cocktail
Garlic Mussels
Smoked Salmon on Homemade Brown Bread
Liver Pate

MAIN COURSE

Fillet of Beef with a Pepper Sauce
Fillet of Wild Salmon with a Hollandaise Sauce
Wild Guinea Fowl with a Red Wine Jus
Spring Lamb with a Mint Sauce
Lobster Thermidor

All main courses are served with a selection of fresh market vegetables and potatoes.

DESSERT

Lemon Sorbet
Black Forest Gateau
Profiteroles with a Chocolate Sauce
Baked Alaska

TEA or COFFEE

1. Type in the menu using centred justification. Choose a nice font. Save the document as MENU.
2. The manageress has forgotten to include the name of the hotel and the date. Insert 'HOTEL DE LUXE' and today's date at the top of the menu.
3. She also forgot the price! Add in the price (£20.00) at the bottom of the menu and insert a reminder that service charge is not included in the price.
4. Don't forget to save your work again.

Business Letters

When typing a business letter you must be extra careful with regard to spelling and punctuation. Normally there is no punctuation in the address, salutation (Dear John part), or closure (Yours faithfully part). The business address is usually written on headed paper with the company logo (design), so there is no need to retype it. Before you start your letter, it is important to leave space for the headed paper (also called a letterhead). Do this by pressing ENTER a few times. In this way, the text won't appear on top of the letterhead when you print. The following is an example of a business letter.

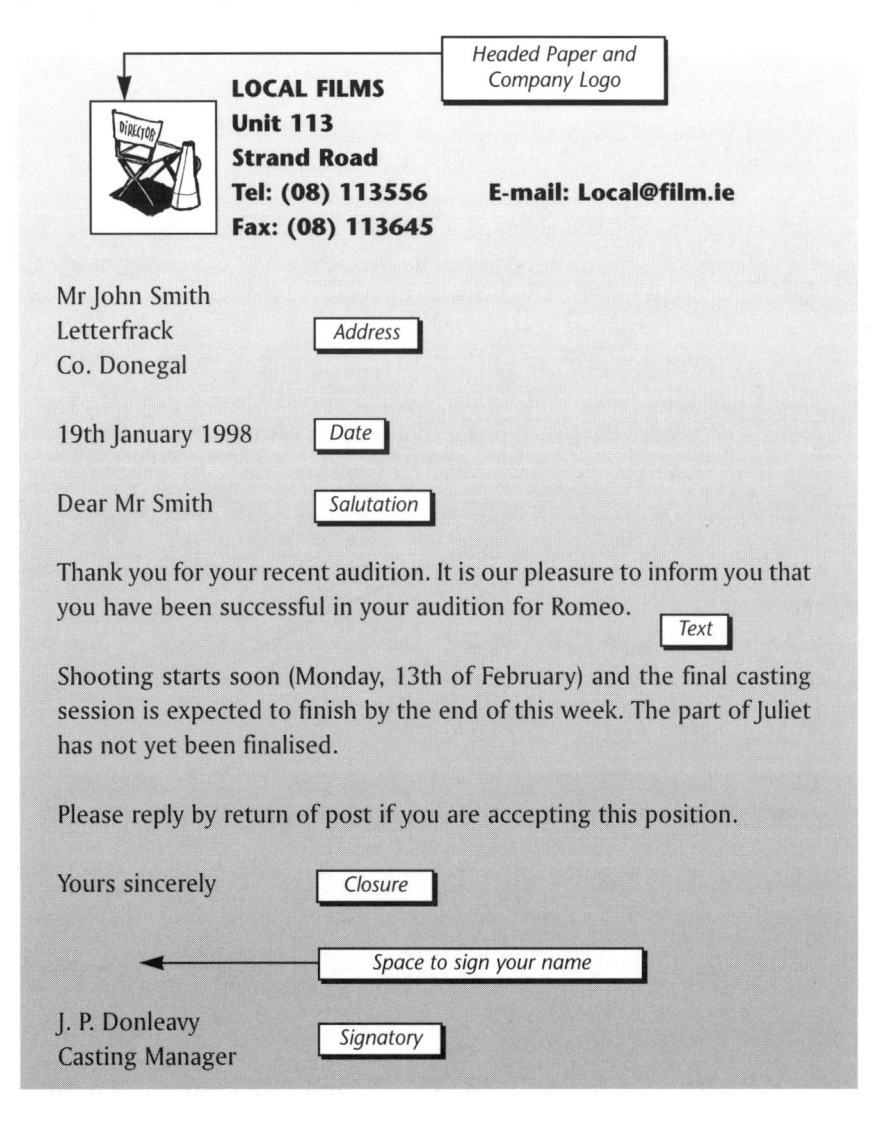

LOCAL FILMS
Unit 113
Strand Road
Tel: (08) 113556 E-mail: Local@film.ie
Fax: (08) 113645

Headed Paper and Company Logo

Mr John Smith
Letterfrack   *Address*
Co. Donegal

19th January 1998   *Date*

Dear Mr Smith   *Salutation*

Thank you for your recent audition. It is our pleasure to inform you that you have been successful in your audition for Romeo.   *Text*

Shooting starts soon (Monday, 13th of February) and the final casting session is expected to finish by the end of this week. The part of Juliet has not yet been finalised.

Please reply by return of post if you are accepting this position.

Yours sincerely   *Closure*

Space to sign your name

J. P. Donleavy
Casting Manager   *Signatory*

For You To Do

Type the above letter in the manner shown. Leave space at the top for the headed paper and also leave space (about 7 or 8 lines) between the closure and the signatory.

Assignment no. 15 This time you are writing a formal letter of complaint regarding a recent cinema visit that went disastrously wrong!

Your Name
Your Address

The Manager
Local Cinemas Inc.

Today's Date

Dear Sir/Madam

I am writing to complain about a recent visit to your cinema. My friends and I decided to go to your cinema on Wednesday last to see the new film.

We were asked to pay £4.50 each. This is the normal fee. We, however, had student cards which entitled us to a 50% discount (a saving of £2.25 each). The ticket operator refused to give us a discount. We showed our student cards to the ticket operator but we were still refused a reduction.

We later discovered that some of our friends were given a discount and they didn't even have their student cards with them! We asked to speak to the manager on duty but we were told that he/she was busy. This is no way to treat customers. Neither my friends nor I will ever return to your cinema for fear of being humiliated in this way again.

We now demand a refund or complimentary tickets. A letter of apology would also go a long way to soothing our anger.

Yours sincerely

Your Name

1. Enhance the letter as you see fit.
2. Change the justification to FULL.
3. Increase the size of the text so that it fills out the page.
4. Save the document as CINEMA.

In this assignment you are applying for a summer job.

Assignment no. 16

Your Name
Your Address

The Manager
Clothes R Us
Daisy Industrial Estate
Cork

Today's Date

Dear Sir/Madam
I am a secondary school student and I am currently applying for summer work. I enclose my C.V. and references.

As you will see from my C.V., I have worked in a variety of summer jobs, including baby-sitting and as a shop assistant in the local shop.

I would like to be considered for any position which may arise in your factory during the summer months. I look forward to hearing from you.

Yours sincerely

Your Name

This is a typical cover letter. It shouldn't be enhanced. It is 'short and sweet', polite and gets the message across in a few short sentences.

It draws attention to your C.V. (more about that later) and informs the reader that there should be both a C.V. and references enclosed. You could add 'Enc.' at the bottom of the page to indicate that something is enclosed with the letter. Cover letters are very important when applying for a job. They can influence whether a C.V. will be read or thrown in the bin. One sure way of giving a bad impression is to have plenty of spelling mistakes in your letter. Sometimes even one mistake is all it takes!

Proofreading and Spelling Checks

Most word processing packages have a built-in spelling checker which can detect and correct many spelling mistakes. There are, however, many errors that it may not detect, for example, *i* instead of *I*, *their* instead of *there*, etc. It is good practice, therefore, to proofread a document by eye before using the spelling checker.

Check the following ten sentences for errors that a spelling checker would miss.

> There clothes were to big and didn't fit them.
> I just love piece and quiet but I rarely have the time to enjoy it.
> Mt. Everest is hire than Mt. Errigal.
> The son always shines in summer when it's warm.
> 'Just give me too minutes to get ready.'
> She doesn't need glasses because she has good site.
> Could you please arrange an other booking?
> He is two busy to answer the telephone.
> Now i no how to correct mistakes!
> Their was a huge sail at the supermarket.

No. of Mistakes Spotted	Score
13	Excellent
12	Good
11	Fair

Try to develop the habit of proofreading by eye before using the spelling checker. It can only check the spelling of words, it cannot make sense of a sentence. Take the following example:

A. The big balloon was swept away by the wind.
B. The big balloon was swept away by the bind.

It's clear in this instance that sentence A makes sense and sentence B does not. However, the word 'bind' is spelled correctly in sentence B. So even though the sentence doesn't make any sense, the spelling checker won't spot the mistake.

Professional proofreaders (people who make a living from spotting mistakes!) read a document backwards. This is because the brain can play tricks. When you read a sentence, you are inclined to predict the next word and insert words or letters where there are none. By reading backwards, it is more difficult to predict the next word and you are less likely to miss a mistake. Try it!

The following passage contains a number of glaring mistakes! See if you can spot them. The number of mistakes in each paragraph is shown to give you some extra help.

Assignment no. 17

I went to the cinema last nite to see a filum. It started at 8.10 p.m. precisly and their was a huge queue at the door. The doorman wasn't going to let me in. He said the cinema was ful, but eventually i got in. ← **6 mistakes**

The smel of popcorn was unberable. Soon the lites went down, the screen went black and the credits started to roll. The music was so loud I thought my ears would pop! ← **3 mistakes**

Act 1 scene 1 started with a earthquake, a car chase and a bank robery. You can imagine what the rest of the film was like! I soon fell asleep and my snoring offended other cinem goers. My money would have been better spent on a good book. ← **3 mistakes**

So, the next day I bought a good book. Well, it was good to start with but the number of spelling mistakes and 'typos' in it soon began to irritate me!

Check the following passage for errors. Apart from spelling, look out for spacing, capitalisation and correct usage of their/there.

Assignment no. 18

Dear Ms Molloy

Thank you for you recent enquiry regarding the new houseing development in you're area. Their will be approximatly 250 new houses built over the next six months.

The scheme will consist of a mixture of 3-bed semi-detached, 4-bed detached and 3/4 bedroom bugalows. Planing permission has been secured.

Bookings are being accepted off the plans. It is anticipated that the houses will be a commecial success so early booking is advisable. Once again, thank you for your interest.

Yours sincerely

Brain Carthy

How many did you catch? There are nine mistakes. If you have time, type in the corrected version of this letter and save it as HOUSE.

Page Set-Up

The way a page is set up involves two important features: *margins* and *orientation*. Let's look at these in more detail.

Margins A margin is the white space between the edge of the page and the text. There are four margins on a page: top, bottom, left and right. These can be adjusted to give a different look to your page. Margins are usually measured in inches or centimetres. The shaded area in the diagram below represents text and the white areas are the margins.

Orientation Orientation refers to the direction of the page. There are two types of orientation: PORTRAIT (lengthways) and LANDSCAPE (widthways). Portrait is the most common.

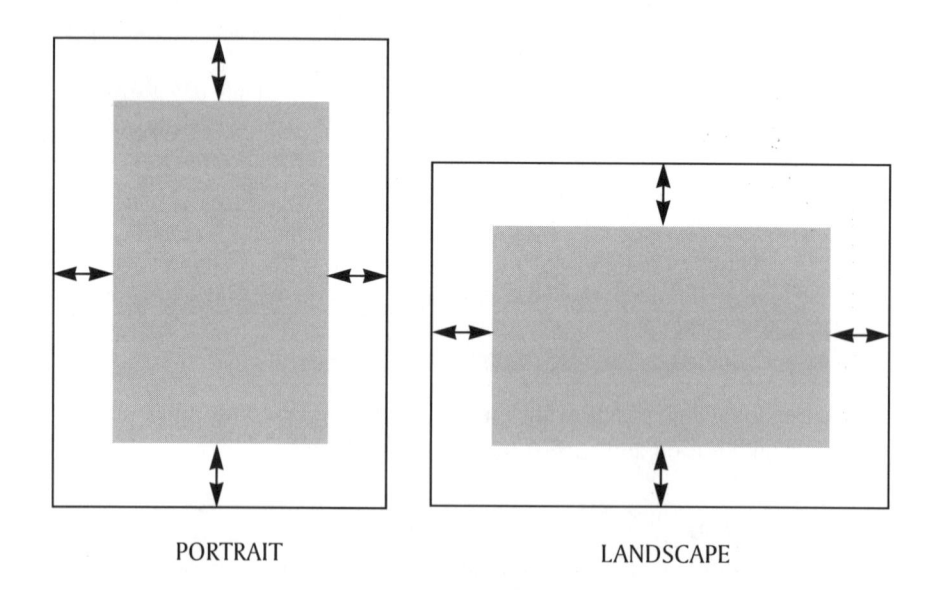

PORTRAIT   LANDSCAPE

For You To Do

Find out how to set margins in your particular word processing application. Retrieve the file HOUSE and change all the margins to 2 inches. You should see the changes on your screen—the text will have adjusted slightly.

Next try to print a page using the different orientations.

The FIND/REPLACE facility is an important tool in word processing. It allows us to seek out any word and replace it automatically with another word throughout the document.

Find and Replace

Type in the following passage and save it as BOAT.

Assignment no. 19

Mr J. Greene
Blackthorn Cottages
Tralee
Co. Kerry

Today's Date

Dear Mr Greene
Thank you for your recent enquiry regarding our new sinkproof dingy, the Titanic. The Titanic has been developed over a number of years to withstand some of the toughest conditions on inland waterways.
The new Titanic has been shaped and modified to withstand force 8 gales and cannot capsize even in these conditions.
Prices for the Titanic are as follows:
Titanic 11'   £256
Titanic 13'   £300
Titanic 15'   £350
Each Titanic comes with an outboard engine and back-up oars. For your information, we are offering a 10% discount on each new Titanic bought before the end of August.
I look forward to hearing from you soon.

Yours sincerely

John Black

1. Change 'Titanic' to 'Dinky' using FIND/REPLACE.
2. Save your document again.

Assignment no. 20 Type in the following passage and carry out the instructions below.

> MARINE ADVENTURE CENTRE
>
> The new Marine Adventure Centre has lots to offer families visiting this part of Ireland. Whether you like hill-walking or water skiing, there's plenty to do. Our plush new cabins offer every comfort to the adventurous traveller. Some cabins even have a sauna and jacuzzi!
>
> Marine Adventure Centre activities include sailing, jet-skiing, scuba diving, water-skiing and power boats, all at very competitive prices to suit your budget.
>
> Certified Marine Adventure Centre instructors will provide detailed instruction in a safe environment.

1. Enhance the text as you see fit.
2. Centre and underline the heading.
3. Make the left margin 1.5 inches wide.
4. Change 'Marine Adventure Centre' to 'PowerSport Adventure Centre'.
5. Change the second paragraph to centre justified.
6. Check the spelling and correct any mistakes.
7. Save the document as POWER.

Assignment no. 21 Type in the text below and carry out the instructions given.

> HOME-MADE ORGANIC PRODUCE FOR SALE
>
> Fresh from the farmhouse. All our produce is made using berries grown organically on the farm. No artificial fertilisers are used on our fields. No artificial preservatives are used in our produce. Everything is completely organic.
>
> BLACKBERRY JAM   only £1.50
> BRAMBLEBERRY JAM   only £1.50
> STRAWBERRY JAM   only £1.00
>
> Be quick! We usually sell out within two days!

1. Save this document as JAM.
2. Replace 'produce' with 'jam'.
3. Centre and embolden the heading.
4. Print one copy.

Tabulation

Tabulation refers to the way we can make text 'jump' a number of spaces across the screen. These jumps are called *tabs* and they are most often used when working with columns of numbers or text. It is easier to align text using tabs than using the spacebar which is inefficient and wastes time. Text aligned using the spacebar can look straight on screen but it usually prints out crooked.

Example A – text aligned using the spacebar

Salesman	Region	Sales
Johnson	A	1200
Murphy	B	1345
Maguire	C	1400

Note the crooked columns. This looks ugly and it takes longer to do.

Example B – text aligned using tabs

Salesman	Region	Sales
Johnson	A	1200
Murphy	B	1345
Maguire	C	1400

Note the straight columns. This looks great and is much quicker to do.

Tabs are normally preset but you can change them easily. Tabs are measured in either inches or centimetres.

Locate the TAB key on your keyboard (it's usually above CAPS LOCK). Find out how to make your own tabs. Find out how to delete tabs. When you are familiar with adding and deleting tabs, try to recreate the table shown below (you don't need to set or delete tabs, just press the tab button to go to another column).

The result of today's matches are as follows:

ARSENAL	1	LIVERPOOL	2
NEWCASTLE	0	MAN. UTD.	0
LEEDS UTD.	2	MAN. CITY	0
QPR	2	ASTON VILLA	2
BLACKBURN	1	CHELSEA	0
FULHAM	0	WIMBLEDON	0

For You To Do

Don't use the spacebar to align text, use the TAB key. This will help you tabulate your text easily.

Assignment no. 22 You have to produce a notice for the staff noticeboard. Type in the information shown below, arranging the four columns of text as shown. Set your tabs in the following positions:

Set the first tab 1.5 inches from the left margin;
Set the second tab 2.5 inches from the left margin;
Set the third tab 4.0 inches from the left margin;
Set the fourth tab 5.0 inches from the left margin.

NOTICE BOARD

The following report details the company sales figures for the first quarter of 1997. Well done to all involved.

Sales for 1997 (first quarter)

Month	Region	Salesman	Sales
January	A	Murphy	1233
February	A	Jones	1022
March	A	Slattery	1304
January	B	Murphy	1300
February	B	Jones	1289
March	B	Slattery	1455
January	C	Murphy	1189
February	C	Jones	1264
March	C	Slattery	1378
January	D	Murphy	1145
February	D	Jones	1388
March	D	Slattery	1377

As you can see from the above figures, this has been an exceptional quarter for the company.

The annual company outing will take place on the 17th of June. Book your place early!

1. Save the document as SALES.
2. Change the right margin to 1.5 inches.
3. Enhance the heading and centre it.
4. Underline the report headings (Month, Region, etc.).
5. Embolden the 'Month' and 'Sales' columns.
6. Make the 'Salesman' column italic.
7. Proofread the document on screen and then use the spelling checker.
8. Correct any errors, save again, and print out one copy in landscape mode.

A shopkeeper is making a list of the goods being included in the summer sale. **Assignment no. 23**
Both the old retail price and the new (discounted) retail price must be listed.
Set tabs at 3.0, 5.0 and 6.0 inches. Enhance the text as you see fit.

SUMMER SALE NOW ON!
Summer madness has started already and this sale must be one of the maddest. How do we do it! Just look at the prices below.

ITEM	WAS	NOW
Beans	30p	20p
Coffee	£1.15	90p
Washing Powder	£2.60	£1.99
Bread	70p	50p

This sale is for one week only and cannot be repeated.

In this exercise you are to set tabs at 1.5, 2.4 and 3.4 inches and key in the data **Assignment no. 24**
below. Ignore subjects that don't apply to you.

JUNIOR CERTIFICATE

SUBJECT	LEVEL	GRADE
IRISH		
ENGLISH		
MATHEMATICS		
HISTORY		
GEOGRAPHY		
FRENCH		
SCIENCE		
MUSIC		
HOME EC.		
BUS. STUDIES		

1. Input the level and grade (or expected grade) that applies to you.
2. Embolden the sub-headings (subject, level and grade).
3. Set left and right margins at 1.5 inches.
4. Make the 'Subject' column bold.
5. Make the 'Grade' column italic.
6. Check for errors.
7. Save the file as SUBJECT.
8. Print out one copy.

Assignment no. 25 In this exercise you will prepare a Curriculum Vitae for a summer job. Follow the format shown below and then input the relevant information.

Curriculum Vitae

PERSONAL DETAILS

NAME:

ADDRESS:

DATE OF BIRTH:

TELEPHONE NUMBER:

EDUCATION
Secondary School 19xx–19yy
    Junior Certificate
        Subject   Level   Grade

WORK EXPERIENCE

INTERESTS AND HOBBIES

REFEREES

First, type in the headings and save the document as CV. Then enhance the headings. In the example shown above, the headings are bold and the first letter of each word is slightly bigger. You can copy the Junior Certificate information directly from your previous assignment.

When typing in your details, remember to tab across. A completed C.V. is shown overleaf. DO NOT over-enhance your C.V. Some companies scan them in to their computer and ask that little or no formatting be used.

Curriculum Vitae

Sample C.V.

Personal Details

NAME: Jane Ferry

ADDRESS: 1 St Johns Road
Donegal Town

DATE OF BIRTH: 01/02/1984

TELEPHONE NUMBER: (074) 1234567

Education

Secondary School 1995 – present
Junior Certificate

SUBJECT	LEVEL	GRADE
IRISH	H	C
ENGLISH	H	B
MATHEMATICS	O	A
HISTORY	H	B
GEOGRAPHY	O	C
FRENCH	H	B
SCIENCE	H	A
BUS. STUDIES	H	A

Work Experience

I have worked as a cashier in the local supermarket for the past two summers. I also have baby-sitting experience.

Interests and Hobbies

I enjoy swimming and I hold a Certificate in Lifesaving (Stage One). I also have a keen interest in drama and I have played the lead role in the school musical.

Referees

Mrs Merton
1 Briar Road
Donegal Town
(074) 2345678

Mr Leamy
Manager
Super-Market
(074) 3456789

Proofreading Symbols

You may at some point want to change your document or, perhaps more commonly, someone may recommend that you change your document! Rather than writing lots of instructions on your printout, symbols will be used to indicate what should be changed. Some of these symbols are shown below.

In the next few exercises you have to create files and carry out the corrections according to the proofreading symbols. Usually, the symbol appears in the margin as well as in the text. This makes it easier to understand the change. So familiarise yourself with these symbols before moving on.

SYMBOL IN MARGIN	MEANING	SYMBOL IN TEXT
ʌ	insert text	the dog went over the ʌwall (high)
⌒|	delete text	⌒| the |small| dog went over the wall
≡	change to capital letters	≡ ⓟaris is the capital of France
╪	change to lower case	Lima is the capital of Peⓡ ╪
⌐	start a new paragraph	The end of the line. ⌐Another part
[ ]	centre	[ACCOUNTS for 1998]
~~	make bold	I was ~~~very~~~ angry
⊔⊓	transpose characters	Park⊔ni⊓g is easy to spell!
Y	insert space	The dogYran after the cat.

Go through the following text noting the symbols and what they mean. Refer to the table above if you get stuck.

A RAINY DAY

≡ It was a rainy day in ⓜay when he fiʌst came across the city. It rose ʳʌ
⌐ up in the distance like a shinhnig jewel. He pondered on his next course of action. Should he go straight in to the city and confront his enemies or would he bide his timeYand enter the city at night- Y fall. He decided on the latter. He felt hungry now. At least there were a few rolls of bread left and some chicken that he had stolen earlier. A Ⓢmile crept across his face as he remembered the ╪ farmer's face! That was a close call.

Create the file GARLIC below and carry out the corrections indicated.

Assignment no. 26

RECIPE FOR GARLIC MUSSELS

INGREDIENTS

1 dozen mussels
2 cloves of garlic
some lemon juice
cream
white wine
seasoning
breadcrumbs

PREPARATION

Wash and scrub mussels thoroughly in cold clean water. Remove 'beards' from the shell. Discard any mussels that are open.

COOKING MUSSELS

Place clean mussels in a large frying pan over a medium/hot heat for approximately 5 minutes. Cover the pan with a lid while cooking. The mussels will cook in their own juices. Discard any mussels that have failed to open. Strain the juices through a muslin cloth to remove any grit or sand. TO MAKE THE SAUCE Add a few tablespoons of the strained juices to half a cup of white wine. Peel and crush the garlic and add to the sauce. Add some lemon juice and seasoning to taste. Spoon this sauce over the mussels and finally coat with breadcrumbs. Grill for a few minutes until the crumbs are golden brown. Eat with lots of wheaten scone to soak up the juice!

Assignment no. 27 Create this review of an Oasis concert and carry out the corrections as shown.

REVIEW

Oasis at the Point

Last night was a nihgt I will never forget. The band were on top form. The ticket, which were priced at £18.00, weren't cheap but money's no object to hear a performance like this. Oasis were supported by the legendary Joe Dolan who gave a magnificent performance.

The crowd packed in to the Point Depot last night to hear their old favourites and they weren't disappointed. Dolan started the night swinging with his famous renditon of "Beautiful Woman". The crowd were exstatic, and this from a supporting act! All too soon his act finished but Dolan returned on to the stage for no less than eight encores. By the time the lead act, Oasis, entered, I'm sure they were wondering who the crowd really came to see. They had a hard act to follow but follow it they certainly did. They started the night with their now famous "Roll With It" but the pace rapidly picked up and soon the crowd were really boogying. The Gallagher boys can really sing! This concert was definitely worth £18.00. See these guys before they leave town.

(Oasis are playing for two more nights only and ticket are nearly sold out.)

Speed Tests

Do the following speed tests to estimate your typing speed in words per minute (w.p.m.). Allow five minutes for each test. The number of words is given beside each line. Remember, accuracy is just as important as speed. There is no point being able to type 40 w.p.m. if your work contains lots of mistakes—three minor mistakes are allowed! Wait until you are given the instruction before commencing typing. Good luck!

Speed Test 1

Words	Text
13	Welcome to this the first edition of the sailing club newsletter. We had
21	a tremendous response to our advertisement requesting new
33	members and, as a result, our membership has now increased to over
47	500! In the coming months, we will be visiting an old shipwreck off the
61	Galway coast. This ship is one of the very few Armada ships to remain
74	in a fairly good condition today. If any of you can scuba-dive, then
87	bring your snorkelling gear along. It promises to be a very good day.
102	The cost of this trip will be in the region of £50. This includes travel,
113	accommodation and food. Not a bad price, I'm sure you'll agree.
126	Please book before 11th April as places are limited. A receipt will be
136	issued on payment. We look forward to seeing you there!

How did you do? To calculate your speed in words per minute, divide the total number of words you typed by five. If you achieved a speed of more than 15 w.p.m., then you are doing really well. The average at this stage is approximately 10 w.p.m. There's plenty more to try on the following pages!

Speed Test 2

Words	Text
13	News leaked out today that a lioness escaped from Dublin zoo in the
24	early hours of Saturday morning. The lioness has been seen stalking
34	some well-known beauty spots but Gardaí are reluctant to say
45	whether she is dangerous, preferring instead to say "any wild animal
59	has a certain degree of danger attached to them and this one is no
68	different". However, a spokesman from the zoo stated categorically
78	that the lioness was indeed dangerous saying, "this particular lioness
89	has come from the deepest jungle and rumours abound that she
98	attacked and killed a man once, before coming here".
112	Lions do not normally eat humans, but if they are old and hungry, they
127	have been known to do so. This is because the lion may not have the
140	strength or speed to kill its normal prey, such as a gazelle. Humans
144	are easier to catch!
157	How can the zoo's statement and that of the Gardaí be so contradictory?
171	It could have something to do with the day that's in it, April 1!

Speed Test 3

12	Advertising is an important area of growth in the Irish economy. Many
24	large firms spend more than £2m each year on advertising. The main
34	advertisers include some of the biggest corporate names in Irish
45	industry, e.g., Guinness, Proctor & Gamble, Lever Bros., etc. Why do
54	businesses spend this amount every year? Does advertising work?
59	Let's look at the following:
72	1. Television is a very attractive medium to advertisers. It is a totally
84	passive medium, i.e., the viewer has to do no work to assimilate
85	information.
96	2. Many people (or targets) watch this medium and advertisers can
107	predict who will watch what and when they will watch it.
119	3. Other media, such as newspapers and radio, are also very attractive
123	to the advertising industry.
134	Does it work? Have you ever heard of a poor advertiser!

Speed Test 4

15	Human beings are made up of cells. A cell is a tiny unit, only visible
28	under a microscope. The control centre of a cell is called the nucleus.
37	The nucleus contains DNA, the genetic material which determines
51	what we look like. A cell also contains a lot of watery fluid called
60	cytoplasm. The cytoplasm has many sugars, proteins and vitamins
72	dissolved in it. Surrounding the cell is a cell membrane. This gives
79	some sort of shape to the cell.
90	There are two major differences between plant cells and animal cells.
104	Firstly, plant cells have a cell wall in addition to a cell membrane. This
117	cell wall gives strength to the cell. The second difference is that plant
127	cells contain chloroplasts. These enable them to make food from
128	sunlight.

Speed Test 5

12	Michael Collins was born in 1890, in Clonakilty, and died 32 years
27	later, in 1922, when he was shot at Beal na mBlath in Co. Cork. He
40	played an enormous part in Irish history. He was involved in the 1916
51	Easter Rising, the War of Independence (1919–20), and the Civil War.
65	Perhaps it is for his role in the War of Independence that Collins is
77	best remembered. He was the most wanted man in the British Empire,
86	yet he successfully evaded capture throughout this period. Eventually,
98	Collins was sent to negotiate a peace settlement in London. When he
110	signed the Treaty, he said, 'I have signed my own death warrant'.
116	These were to prove prophetic words.

Fun With Word Processing

It is quite easy to make up brochures, advertisements, questionnaires, invitations and cards in your word processing application. Sometimes this is called *desktop publishing*. All it takes is a little imagination.

Design

Design is very important when it comes to desktop publishing. You should try to visualise what you want to create before you start. Who is it aimed at? A birthday card for a friend will look totally different to a card for a wedding! Don't go overboard with fancy fonts and borders. These can kill a design. Keep it simple.

Art

It is easy to add art to your document. Most word processing applications come with 'clip art' supplied. If not, you can easily create some simple graphics in a painting application and bring these in (import them) to your document. You may even have access to a professional desktop publishing application (like Pagemaker or QuarkXPress). This makes it even easier to create brochures, cards, etc. Some fonts consist of symbols that are art-based, e.g., ✂ ✈ ❐. Check your word processor for a font like this.

Borders can improve the layout of a document. However, they can also distract the reader from the central message you are trying to convey. Use them with discretion.

This is a simple example of desktop publishing. We are going to make a cut-out coupon. The airplane is a clip art image. The scissors icon is part of a font.

For You To Do

✂- -

FLY TO DISNEYWORLD COMPETITION

To enter this competition, simply answer this question.

Question: What city is nearest Disneyworld in Florida?

Answer: _____

Now fill in your name and address and complete the tie-breaker in 10 words or less. That's all there is to it and you could be flying to Disneyworld this summer!

NAME _____
ADDRESS _____
_____

Tie-breaker: I want to go to Disneyworld because ... _____
_____

Questionnaire

This is a typical questionnaire used for surveys. You have probably filled in one like it yourself. The box (❏) and the tick (✓) are taken from a font. Try making it yourself on your word processing application.

QUESTIONNAIRE

Please answer each question by placing a tick (✓) in the appropriate box. Your answers are confidential.

CLASS: **AGE:**

1. How much pocket money do you get each week?
    - ❏ £5 or less
    - ❏ £10 or less
    - ❏ more than £10

2. How often do you go to the cinema?
    - ❏ less than once a week
    - ❏ once a week
    - ❏ more than once a week

3. How long do you spend on homework each night?
    - ❏ less than one hour
    - ❏ less than two hours
    - ❏ more than two hours

4. Have you ever been to a concert?
    - ❏ YES   ❏ NO

5. Have you ever gone abroad?
    - ❏ YES   ❏ NO

THANK YOU FOR ANSWERING THESE QUESTIONS!

This card is printed on standard A4 paper. Print both pages in LANDSCAPE orientation. After printing the first page, insert it in to the printer again and print the second page. Now you should have text on both sides of the paper. Fold the page in half and send it off!

Valentine's Day Card

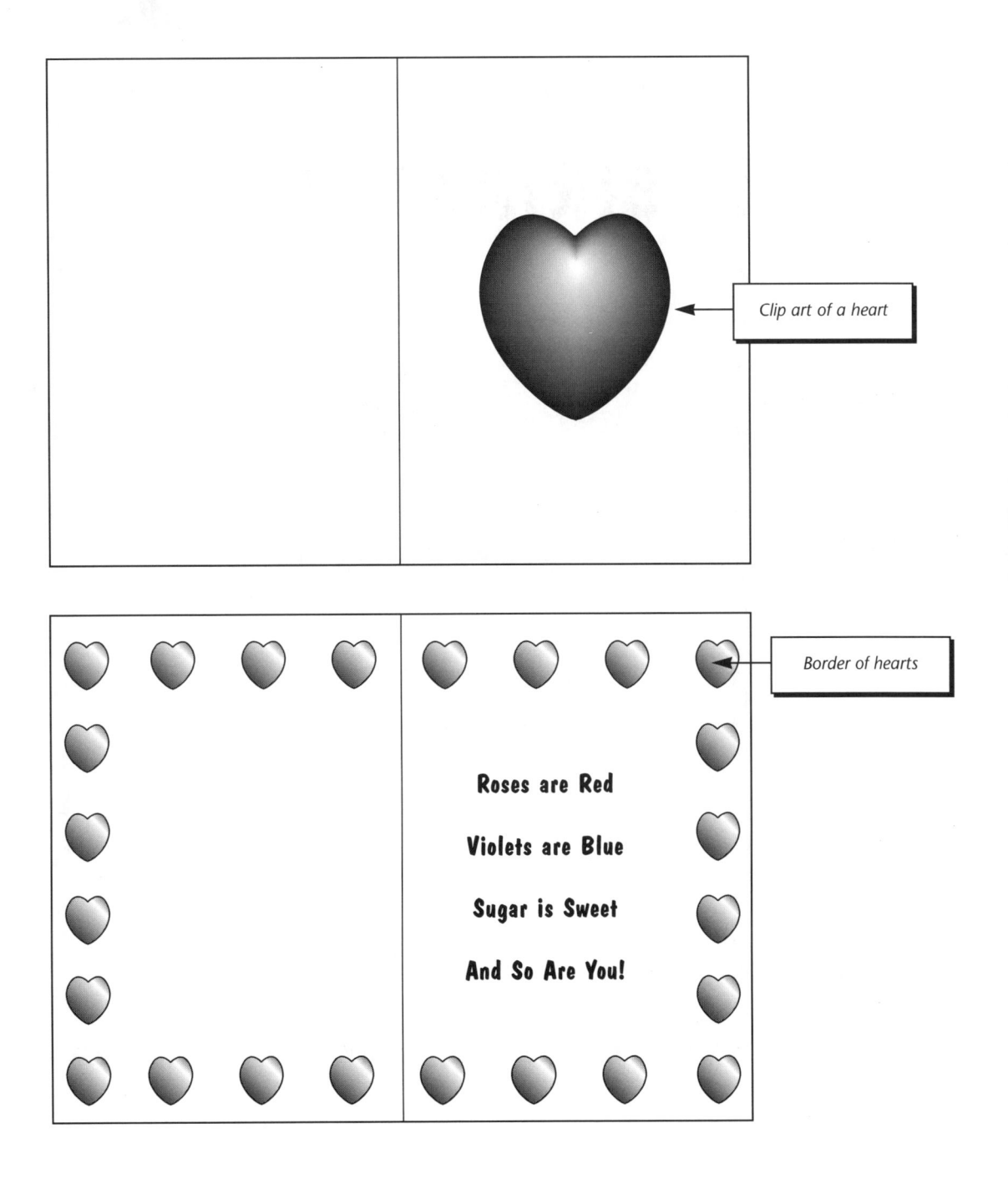

Clip art of a heart

Border of hearts

Roses are Red

Violets are Blue

Sugar is Sweet

And So Are You!

Invitation

Invitations are easy to make. The invitation below is for a birthday party and it is printed on A4 paper. The cake is taken from a collection of clip art, as is the border. You can make this even more attractive by printing it on coloured paper which you should find in most stationery suppliers.

BIRTHDAY PARTY

You are invited to attend my
15th birthday party

on

Saturday 12th June at 3.00 p.m.

Call me if you can't make it!
Niamh (045) 123456

Newsletter

It is beyond the scope of this book to go in to the finer details of desktop publishing. There are numerous books already available on the subject if you are interested. However, here are a few tips and ideas on the subject of publishing a newsletter or a yearbook.

Template

You may be involved in a club or society at school that produces a regular newsletter. If so, it is a good idea to produce a *template* (master document) that can be used over and over again. Within the template, areas are assigned for headings, text, art or pictures. This saves you having to redesign your newsletter each time a new edition comes out and also ensures that the 'look' of the document is consistent. The different areas of your template are sometimes called *frames*. Each contributor to the newsletter can type up their text, save it and give it to the person who is compiling the publication. After that, it is a simple matter of cutting and pasting in to the different frames.

HEADING FRAME		CLIP ART
TEXT COLUMN 1	TEXT COLUMN 2	TEXT BOX
		PHOTO OR CLIP ART

Research

Research is vital for any publication. You must make sure that the information you are publishing is accurate. You can check your facts using an encyclopaedia, newspaper articles, by calling people, writing to people or organisations and, of course, using the Internet.

Editor

You should also decide on an editor for your newsletter. This person will check the facts, spelling and the length of each article.

Compiler

Only one person should compile the publication. This will make the publishing process more efficient. Four or five students gathered around one computer won't make the newsletter appear any quicker and will probably slow down the whole operation. A sample page of a newsletter is shown overleaf—try recreating it!

Sample Newsletter Here is a sample page of a school newsletter. The heading and text frames are contained within a template which can be used repeatedly. This will ensure consistency in all future editions of the newsletter. Once the template is prepared, all you have to do is input the text and graphics.

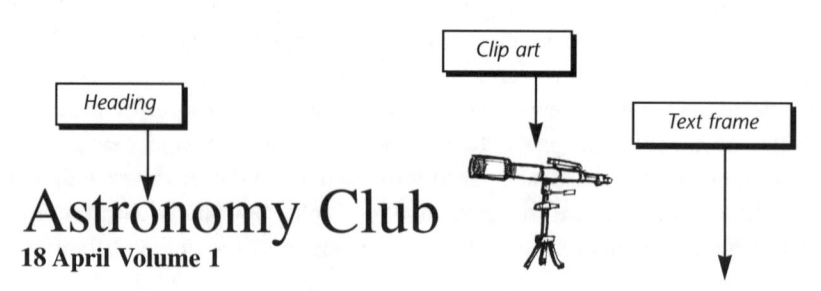

Heading →

Clip art →

Text frame →

Astronomy Club
18 April Volume 1

This is the first issue of the new Astronomy Club newsletter. In this issue, we look at the Moon and Mars, both of which are visible in the sky right now.

The Astronomy Club has over thirty members from first year to sixth year. We meet every Monday at 4.00 p.m. If the sky is clear, we will do some sky gazing. If not, there will be a slide show. We hope to visit the Planetarium in Armagh and the Dunsink Observatory during the school year. Copies of *Astronomy Ireland* are available to read. Ask Alison for details.

IN THIS ISSUE
TELESCOPES
BINOCULARS
LETTERS
MOON FACTS
MARS FACTS
WHERE TO LOOK

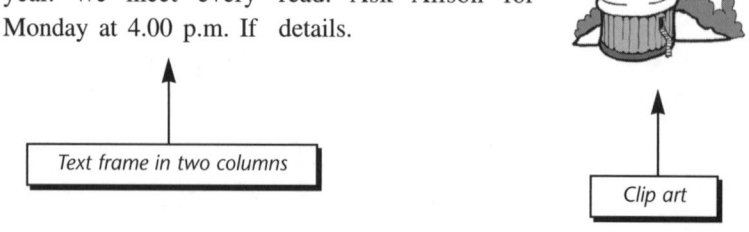

↑ *Text frame in two columns*

↑ *Clip art*

Assessment Log Book

TASK	METHOD	DATE/SIGNATURE
The history of the computer	Oral	
Understand the 4-stage model	Oral, Written Test	
Understand the different keys	Assignment Nos. 1, 2	
Inputting text	Assignment Nos. 1, 2	
Understand the uses of word processing; advantages/disadvantages	Written Test	
Saving a file	Assignment No. 3	
Inserting/deleting text	Assignment Nos. 4, 5	
Enhancements	Assignment Nos. 6, 7, 8, 9, 10, 11	
Cutting, copying and pasting blocks	Assignment No. 12	
Justification	Assignment Nos. 13, 14	
Business letters	Assignment Nos. 15, 16	
Proofreading and spelling checks	Assignment Nos. 17, 18	
Margins and orientation	Assignment No. 18	
Finding/replacing text	Assignment Nos. 19, 20, 21	
Tabulation	Assignment Nos. 22, 23, 24, 25	
Proofreading symbols	Assignment Nos. 26, 27	
Speed tests	Speed Tests 1, 2, 3, 4, 5	

PART III DATABASES

What is a Database?

A database is a collection of information that is organised in some way. The information is arranged or ordered so that it can be easily retrieved. You've probably used a database already and you didn't even know it! Examples of databases include a library (all the books are organised by subject and by author) and a telephone directory (organised alphabetically by surname). We will look at making databases on a computer.

Where are Databases Used?

Did you ever go in to a bookshop and ask for a particular book? The bookseller probably consulted a computer database before giving you the answer. Databases are used in a wide range of situations: to book flights, to hold details of hospital patients, to store bank account details, in fact nearly everywhere.

Example

NAME	SURNAME	ADDRESS	SEX	DOB
JOHN	MARTIN	1 BLACK ROAD	M	12/08/87
JOAN	BLACK	113 OLD ROAD	F	26/01/88
MARY	MAGUIRE	34 COTTAGE RD	F	01/05/88
PATRICK	MAGUIRE	23 THE GABLES	M	17/03/88

This database contains information on four people and the information is divided in to five sections—first name, surname, address, sex and date of birth. It is a very small database and wouldn't be used in real life because it is too small. Any information you might want from this database is easily found. For example, how many people were born before 1988? The answer is just one. How many people are male? Answer: Two. Therefore, getting information from this database is easy. But what if there were thousands of names in it! This is where a computer is used. Most commercial databases have hundreds or thousands of names, dates, etc. contained within them. To retrieve this information would be incredibly time-consuming without the aid of a computer.

Don't worry though! The databases we will make won't contain hundreds of names or details. It would take too long to input this amount of information. But you will learn to use the full power of the computer when dealing with a database. You will learn to create a database, ask questions by searching for things within it, sort a database, and much more. Let's get started!

Before you make your first database, you must understand two terms: *fields* and *records*. The precise meaning of these terms can be explained if you think of a database in terms of rows and columns.

Fields and Records

All the information in a row is related, e.g., in row 1 of the database shown below, all the information concerns John Martin. This is a *record* for John Martin.

Similarly, each column contains the same type of information, e.g., the DOB column contains dates of birth only. This is called a *field*.

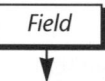

NAME	SURNAME	ADDRESS	SEX	DOB
JOHN	MARTIN	1 BLACK ROAD	M	12/08/87
JOAN	BLACK	113 OLD ROAD	F	26/01/88
MARY	MAGUIRE	34 COTTAGE ROAD	F	01/05/88
PATRICK	MAGUIRE	23 THE GABLES	M	17/03/88

So, in this database there are five fields (NAME, SURNAME, ADDRESS, SEX and DOB) and there are four records (concerning John Martin, Joan Black, Mary Maguire and Patrick Maguire).

The width of a field specifies how much information can be typed in to it. Each character counts as one so the name John is four characters wide. Spaces also count as one character. You must allow for the widest data when determining the width of a field. The DOB field must have a width of eight characters to accommodate the dates because dd/mm/yy is eight characters wide. What field widths are required for the other fields?

Field Width

NAME = 7 (to allow for Patrick, the longest name)
SURNAME = 7 (to allow for Maguire, the longest surname)
ADDRESS = 15 (to allow for 34 Cottage Road)
SEX = 1
DOB = 8

If the following record was added to the database, what field widths would be required?

NAME	SURNAME	ADDRESS	SEX	DOB
MARY-ROSE	O'HANLON	1 COTTAGE ROAD	F	12/09/88

Field Datatype

The datatype of a field refers to the nature of the data within the field. Datatypes can be

- NUMERIC (numbers only)
- ALPHABETIC (letters only)
- DATE (dates only)
- ALPHANUMERIC (both numbers and letters)

The datatype of the NAME field in our sample database is alphabetic.

The design of your database is very important. Imagine the frustration of discovering that you forgot to add a field after you've keyed in all the information! So, **plan your database in advance**, before you begin working on the computer. List the fields that you'll need, the field widths, and the datatype of each field.

> **For You To Do**
>
> Examine the databases below. What are the widths and datatypes of the fields? How many records are there are in each database?

PATIENT	WARD	DOCTOR	DOB
JOHNSON	A	JONES	12/11/88
CAMPBELL	A	HUDSON	05/03/90
WHELAN	B	JONES	19/12/78

NAME	SECTION	SALARY	TEL_NO
HANSON	1	15,000	1134667
GALLAGHER	1	16,000	223668
O'BRIEN	12	13,000	5574328
SCOTT	9	14,000	3357924

> **For You To Do**
>
> Find out the name of the database application you are using and how to open it. Then create either of the databases shown above. Try changing the data in the records and adding in some records of your own. **Always use the same format** when entering data, e.g., don't use 12/02/89 in one record and 12th February 1989 in another.

Create a database using the following field names, widths and datatypes.

Assignment no. 28

FIELD	WIDTH	DATATYPE
NAME	10	ALPHABETIC
DEPARTMENT	10	ALPHABETIC
TEL	7	NUMERIC
DOB	8	ALPHANUMERIC

Then input this additional information in to your database.

NAME	DEPARTMENT	TEL	DOB
ABRAMS	SALES	2233678	12/02/78
WILLIAMS	SALES	2233678	02/06/79
JOHNSON	TECHNICAL	4797653	09/08/80
RAMSEY	CLERICAL	4543874	27/03/78
POWER	TECHNICAL	4797653	17/12/77
MAHER	SALES	2233678	23/06/89
KIERNAN	MARKETING	4623789	12/12/89

1. Save this database as DB1.
2. Add the following records:

NAME	DEPARTMENT	TEL	DOB
MOONEY	TECHNICAL	4755693	12/05/79
MCELWEE	SALES	4623789	18/02/80
Your Name	MARKETING	4623789	Your DOB

3. KIERNAN has changed department—he is now in SALES. Make this change in the database.
4. Change his TELEPHONE number to 2233678.
5. Save again and print out the complete file with the new changes.

Handy Hint

You can view your database as a list of records (as shown above) or you can view it one record at a time. Some people find it easier to input information when there is only one record on screen. This is sometimes called a **DATA INPUT FORM**.

Assignment no. 29 A farmer wants to put some information about his cattle in to a database. He has supplied you with the data shown below. Determine the field widths and datatypes required, and then create this database. Save your file as BEEF.

For You To Do

BREED	COLOUR	USES
CHAROLLAIS	CREAMY WHITE	BEEF
JERSEY	LIGHT BROWN	MILK
FRIESIAN	BLACK AND WHITE	MILK AND BEEF
ABERDEEN ANGUS	BLACK	BEEF
HEREFORD	RED AND WHITE	BEEF
SIMMENTAL	BROWN AND WHITE	MILK AND BEEF
KERRY	BLACK	MILK
SHORTHORN	RED	MILK
HIGHLAND	BLACK	BEEF

The farmer has just returned from the mart with some more cattle. Information on these animals must be added to the database.

1. Add the following records to the file:

BREED	COLOUR	USES
LIMOUSINE	BLACK	BEEF
GUERNSEY	FAWN	MILK
BELGIAN BLUE	BLUE	BEEF

2. Save again and print out the complete file.

Searching Records

One of the most powerful features of databases is the ease with which we can search through them for information. Searches are sometimes called queries or interrogations. It is important that we learn how to search properly.

STEP 1 Know what **field** your information is in.

STEP 2 Know what **information** to seek.

Example

Retrieve the database BEEF. Let's suppose you're looking to find those cattle that are used for beef purposes only. This means your information is located in the USES field. Sometimes this is written as USES=BEEF. In other words, you're asking the computer to search through the USES field and extract only those records containing BEEF. This is called a *single condition search* because we are only looking for one thing. When you carry out this search, you should see the following results on your screen.

BREED	COLOUR	USES
CHAROLLAIS	CREAMY WHITE	BEEF
ABERDEEN ANGUS	BLACK	BEEF
HEREFORD	RED AND WHITE	BEEF
HIGHLAND	BLACK	BEEF
LIMOUSINE	BLACK	BEEF
BELGIAN BLUE	BLUE	BEEF

For You To Do

To answer the following questions, what fields would you search in your database? Write down your answers.

1. How many black cattle are there?
2. What cattle are used for MILK only?
3. What are the uses of the Belgian Blue?
4. What colour is the Friesian?

Now search the database for black cattle. Then search for cattle which produce milk only.

Assignment no. 30 The database below is available at a tourist office. Read through the database to familiarise yourself with it and then try the exercise that follows. 'Greater than' is written as '>' and 'less than' is written as '<'.

HOTEL	ROOMS	RATING	ROOMS_FREE
GRANDE	34	**	10
RIO	50	***	5
MONTRE	200	***	0
RICOS	105	****	20
SUPERIOR	200	*****	0
CARLOS	50	**	40
ROCO	48	***	0
GLADE	60	*	20
SAMBA	30	****	2
SUNNY	10	**	3

To answer the questions below, a search would have to be conducted within the database. Match each question with the correct search. Remember to choose the field the information is contained in first, and then look for the actual information.

QUESTION	SEARCH
1. Which hotels are fully booked?	RATING=**
2. How many 2-star hotels are there?	ROOMS<50
3. Which hotels have more than 50 rooms?	ROOMS_FREE=0
4. Which hotels have less than 50 rooms?	ROOMS>50
5. How many 5-star hotels are there?	RATING=*****

How did you do? Your next task is to create this database and ask those questions. Remember to specify the width and datatype of each field before you start. Save your file as HOTEL and print out one copy.

More Searches

So far we've used three *operators* in our database searches: equals (=), less than (<) and greater than (>). There are several other operators you can use, such as 'NOT EQUALS', 'CONTAINS', 'AND', 'NOT' and 'OR'. (These may be slightly different depending on the application you are using.)

Examples

In your HOTEL database, if you wanted to search for hotels that are not 2-star, you would use '≠**' or 'NOT **'. Similarly, if you were looking for a hotel with the letters CA in its name, then your search would be entered as 'CONTAINS CA'.

The operators 'AND' and 'OR' are used for *multiple condition searches*. For example, if you wanted to find a 3-star hotel with more than 100 rooms, your search would be input as 'RATING=*** **AND** ROOMS>100'. Thus, there are two conditions in this search. The first requirement is that the hotel has a 3-star rating and the second is that it has more than 100 rooms. Only records with both these requirements will be retrieved and displayed.

If you were searching for a 2-star or a 3-star hotel, you would enter 'RATING=** **OR** RATING=***'. In this instance, the computer will retrieve records that fulfil either requirement.

Retrieve the file HOTEL and carry out the following searches.
1. Search for hotels with a 2-star rating.
2. Search for hotels that have more than 40 rooms.
3. Search for 2-star hotels with more than 40 rooms.
4. Search for hotels that contain the letters RI in their name.
5. Search for hotels with a rating of 4 or more stars that are not booked out.
6. Print out the last search only.
7. Save the file and exit.

Assignment no. 31 Here's another database for you to create! In this assignment you are working in a museum, creating an information database on volcanoes which the public will use!

VOLCANO	LOCATION	ERUPTION	HEIGHT
VESUVIUS	ITALY	1944	4230
SANTORINI	GREECE	1950	4316
STROMBOLI	ITALY	1930	3055
HEKLA	ICELAND	1970	4920
ASKJA	ICELAND	1961	4983
LANZAROTE	CANARY ISLANDS	1824	1855
ETNA	ITALY	1974	10855
EREBUS	ANTARCTICA	1947	13200
MAUNA LOA	HAWAII	1997	164000
DECEPTION ISLAND	ANTARCTICA	1970	1890

1. Save your file as VOLCANO.
2. Search for volcanoes in Italy.
3. Search for volcanoes that erupted before 1900.
4. Search for volcanoes in Antarctica that erupted after 1950.
5. Find the highest volcano.
6. Search for volcanoes in Italy that are more than 10,000 ft high.
7. Search for volcanoes in Iceland that erupted during or after 1970.
8. Print out the results of the last search.
9. Print out the complete database.

Sorting Records

Sometimes it is necessary to sort the records of a database in alphabetical order or in numerical order. This is easy to do. Sorts can be arranged in *ascending* or *descending* order.

If the numbers 1 to 10 were sorted in ascending order, they would be arranged as 1, 2, 3, 4, 5, 6, 7, 8, 9, 10. If they were sorted in descending order, they would appear as 10, 9, 8, 7, 6 ... and so on.

Key Field

So, it is easy to sort records—all you have to do is choose the field you want to sort and then sort the records in this field in either ascending or descending order. Any field can be sorted. The field on which the database is sorted is called the *key field*. If you wanted to sort the records of the previous VOLCANO database by location, then the LOCATION field would be the key field.

FIRST_NAME	SURNAME	SEX	POSITION
MARY	BYRNE	F	CASHIER
PAUL	CANNING	M	SECURITY
ENDA	MURPHY	M	CASHIER
MICHAEL	O'HARA	M	SECURITY
EDEL	WATERS	F	MANAGER

EXAMPLE 1 — Sorted in ascending order by surname.

FIRST_NAME	SURNAME	SEX	POSITION
PAUL	CANNING	M	SECURITY
MICHAEL	O'HARA	M	SECURITY
MARY	BYRNE	F	CASHIER
ENDA	MURPHY	M	CASHIER
EDEL	WATERS	F	MANAGER

EXAMPLE 2 — Sorted in descending order by first name.

For You To Do

If you were to carry out the following sorts on the database VOLCANO, what key fields would you use—

1. To list the volcanoes alphabetically?
2. To list the volcanoes according to the year of eruption?
3. To list the volcanoes according to their country?

Find out how to sort records in your database application and carry out these sorts on your VOLCANO file.

Assignment no. 32 The local doctor wants to put some of his patients' details in to a database. You must specify a name, width and datatype for each field, enter the information, and then carry out the instructions below.

For You To Do

FIRSTNAME	SURNAME	SYMPTOMS	DATE	PAID
PAUL	SMITH	SORE THROAT	12/12/97	YES
MARY	MURRAY	PAINS IN LEG	13/12/97	YES
JOHN	COSGRAVE	BROKEN ARM	10/07/97	NO
MICHELLE	ADAMS	SORE THROAT	09/12/97	NO
SANDRA	MURPHY	VERRUCA	19/05/96	NO
HUGH	FRIEL	HEADACHE	28/04/97	YES
DONALD	MACALLUM	NECKACHE	14/08/96	NO
ALAN	SYNNOTT	BACKACHE	23/07/97	YES
CAROL	VAUGHAN	SORE THROAT	13/12/97	YES
JAMES	O'NEIL	SORE FOOT	14/03/96	YES

1. Save this database as DOCTOR.
2. Sort the records alphabetically by SURNAME.
3. Search for patients suffering from a sore throat. (Do you notice anything about the dates?)
4. Add your own record (make it up) and sort the database by DATE.
5. Search for patients who were suffering from a sore throat and who haven't paid yet.
6. Print out a list of those patients who didn't pay for visits in 1996.
7. Save the sorted database as DOCTOR1.

You have been ordered to create the following database for the army! Once again, determine the name, width and datatype for each field and carry out the instructions below. Be careful when entering the data!

Assignment no. 33

FIRST_NAME	SURNAME	SECTION	DATE_IN	ACCESS
ADRIAN	SMITH	INFANTRY	01/06/80	NO
GLENDA	MCCARTHY	INTELLIGENCE	15/08/82	YES
MARY	BOLAND	INFANTRY	23/09/80	NO
JOHN	CLARKE	INTELLIGENCE	28/12/81	YES
MICHAEL	MURPHY	MP	20/09/83	NO
LAURA	WHITE	INFANTRY	24/11/84	NO
JIM	MACALLUM	INTELLIGENCE	15/02/81	NO
SHANE	HOGAN	MP	17/05/80	YES
IVOR	HALL	INTELLIGENCE	19/03/81	YES
NOREEN	O'LOONEY	MP	28/09/84	YES

1. Save this database as ARMY.
2. Sort the records alphabetically by SURNAME.
3. Search for members who are in the INTELLIGENCE section.
4. Add your own record (make it up) and sort the database using the DATE field.
5. Print out a list of those who are allowed access.
6. Who is the most recent recruit?
7. Search for members who are allowed access but are not in the intelligence unit.

Assignment no. 34 A travel agent has discovered that you know how to create databases and has asked for your help. He wants a database containing flight and passenger information which he can search easily. He has given you the following details:

SURNAME	INITIAL	DESTINATION	REF_NO	COST
O'BRIEN	J	LIMA, PERU	PR-1334	£655
WOOD	F	MADRID, SPAIN	SP-M12	£366
SMITH	N	BARCELONA, SPAIN	SP-B13	£378
JONES	T	PARIS, FRANCE	FR-101	£99
BROWN	V	MILAN, ITALY	IT-M32	£199
ANDERSON	E	ROME, ITALY	IT-R11	£234
OWENS	S	ORLANDO, U.S.A.	US-FL988	£399
ROONEY	P	NICE, FRANCE	FR-N223	£156
NELSON	T	NEW YORK, U.S.A.	US-NY34	£299
DEMPSEY	B	MOSCOW, RUSSIA	RU-M266	£499

1. Save this database as TRAVEL.
2. Sort the records alphabetically by SURNAME.
3. Search for flights costing less than £300.
4. Add your own record (make it up) and sort the database using the REF_NO field.
5. Search for flights to the U.S.A.
6. Sort the records according to cost.
7. Search for passengers travelling to Russia.
8. Print out one copy of the database sorted by SURNAME.

You have been fortunate enough to get a summer job in your local hotel. The management were very impressed with your C.V., noting in particular your knowledge of databases. Having just purchased a computer, they decide to computerise their records. This is your job! The manager gives you the following twelve index cards and asks you to put the information in to a database.

Assignment no. 35
Part 1

For You To Do

ROOM_NO 1 BEDS 2 ENSUITE Y DATE_IN 13/07 DATE_OUT 14/07 CHARGE/NIGHT £22.50	ROOM_NO 5 BEDS 4 ENSUITE Y DATE_IN free DATE_OUT free CHARGE/NIGHT £32.50	ROOM_NO 9 BEDS 2 ENSUITE N DATE_IN 17/07 DATE_OUT 23/07 CHARGE/NIGHT £20
ROOM_NO 2 BEDS 1 ENSUITE N DATE_IN 12/07 DATE_OUT 14/07 CHARGE/NIGHT £20.50	ROOM_NO 6 BEDS 4 ENSUITE N DATE_IN 13/07 DATE_OUT 14/07 CHARGE/NIGHT £25	ROOM_NO 10 BEDS 2 ENSUITE N DATE_IN 17/07 DATE_OUT 23/07 CHARGE/NIGHT £20
ROOM_NO 3 BEDS 2 ENSUITE Y DATE_IN free DATE_OUT free CHARGE/NIGHT £22.50	ROOM_NO 7 BEDS 2 ENSUITE Y DATE_IN 10/07 DATE_OUT 14/07 CHARGE/NIGHT £22.50	ROOM_NO 11 BEDS 3 ENSUITE Y DATE_IN 17/07 DATE_OUT 23/07 CHARGE/NIGHT £25
ROOM_NO 4 BEDS 2 ENSUITE Y DATE_IN 13/07 DATE_OUT 20/07 CHARGE/NIGHT £22.50	ROOM_NO 8 BEDS 2 ENSUITE N DATE_IN free DATE_OUT free CHARGE/NIGHT £20	ROOM_NO 12 BEDS 4 ENSUITE Y DATE_IN free DATE_OUT free CHARGE/NIGHT £32.50

Save this database as HOTEL1. Check that the field names, widths and datatypes are correct before going on to Part 2.

Assignment no. 35 Part 2

The hotel management are very impressed with your work so far and want to know what the database can do. They have completed an extension and have added more rooms to the hotel. They want you to add information about these new rooms to the database. Here are the index cards.

ROOM_NO 13	ROOM_NO 15	ROOM_NO 17
BEDS 2	BEDS 2	BEDS 4
ENSUITE Y	ENSUITE Y	ENSUITE Y
DATE_IN free	DATE_IN free	DATE_IN free
DATE_OUT free	DATE_OUT free	DATE_OUT free
CHARGE/NIGHT £25	CHARGE/NIGHT £25	CHARGE/NIGHT £35

ROOM_NO 14	ROOM_NO 16	ROOM_NO 18
BEDS 2	BEDS 4	BEDS 6
ENSUITE Y	ENSUITE Y	ENSUITE Y
DATE_IN free	DATE_IN free	DATE_IN free
DATE_OUT free	DATE_OUT free	DATE_OUT free
CHARGE/NIGHT £25	CHARGE/NIGHT £35	CHARGE/NIGHT £50

The manager asks you to work on the reservations desk for a day. You have to use the database to answer customer queries.

A tourist comes in to the hotel and asks you how many rooms are ensuite.

She then asks about making a reservation on the 23/07. Are there any rooms free?

She wants one room with 4 beds for her family. Are there any available?

She asks if there are any 4-bed rooms costing less than £30 per night available.

Finally, she asks for a printout showing the 4-bed rooms available.

How did you do on the reservations desk?

Handy Hint

You can save searches or queries by naming them. For example, you could save the search for free rooms and call it FREE. You could then run that search over and over again without having to type in the information required each time. This can speed up the searching process considerably if a particular search is performed regularly.

Adding/Deleting Fields

There may be times when you've set up your database but forgotten to add a particular field, or perhaps it contains a field you didn't intend to put in. In these circumstances, you can modify your database by adding or deleting these fields. Find out how to do this in your database application and then try Assignment no. 36.

Assignment no. 36

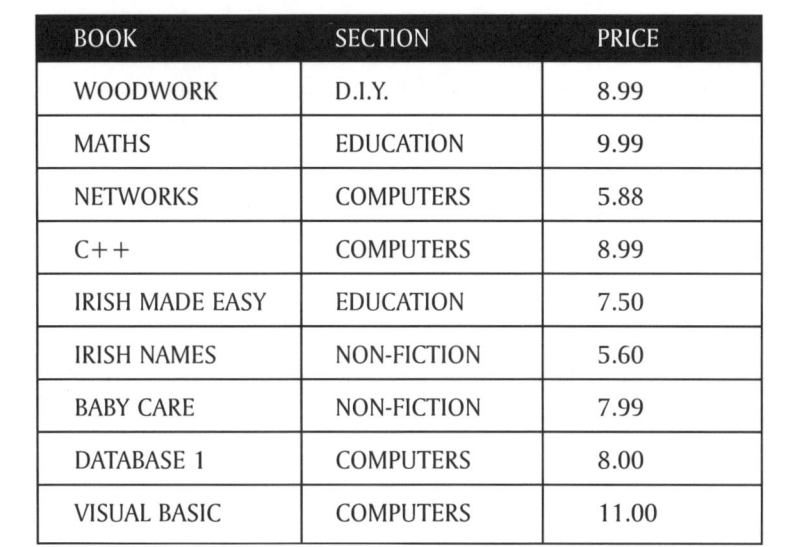

Create the following database for a bookshop. Remember to create names, widths and datatypes for all the fields.

BOOK	SECTION	PRICE
WOODWORK	D.I.Y.	8.99
MATHS	EDUCATION	9.99
NETWORKS	COMPUTERS	5.88
C++	COMPUTERS	8.99
IRISH MADE EASY	EDUCATION	7.50
IRISH NAMES	NON-FICTION	5.60
BABY CARE	NON-FICTION	7.99
DATABASE 1	COMPUTERS	8.00
VISUAL BASIC	COMPUTERS	11.00

For You To Do

1. Save this database as BOOKS.
2. Create a new field called AUTHOR and add the following information: JOHNSON, SHERIDAN, FRIEL, O'HARA, MURPHY, MCELWEE, CAREY, MITCHELL and JONES.
3. Search for books costing less than £7.00.
4. Sort the database alphabetically by AUTHOR.

Written Test

These questions are designed to test your understanding of everything that has been explained so far about databases. Good luck!

1. What is a database?
2. Name three places where you would expect to find a database.
3. Explain the difference between a field and a record.
4. Name three different types of field.
5. What is meant by field width?
6. These records are sorted according to what field?

FIRST NAME	SURNAME	DOB
John	Adams	12/03/89
Jane	Ferry	15/03/80
Mary	Maguire	20/09/85

7. In the records above, which field would you search to find the youngest person?
8. Which of the following operators would you use to find a name containing the letter B?

   A. contains B
   B. < B
   C. > B
   D. > b

9. Which of the following fields would be most useful in a travel agent's database?

   A. arrival time
   B. cost
   C. departure time
   D. clothing

10. Explain the difference between viewing the records in a database as a list and viewing them as individual data input forms.

Using Maths on Fields

A powerful function of most databases is the ability to use maths on fields. This means that fields can be added together, subtracted, multiplied or divided. You can also tell the database to automatically calculate the sum of a field (add up all the values in that field) or to calculate the maximum, minimum, or average value in a field.

Example

PRODUCT	MANUFACTURER	NET	RETAIL	PROFIT
BREAD	LOCAL	0.67	0.78	
BREAD	CO-OP	0.54	0.70	
BUTTER	CO-OP	0.77	0.89	
BUTTER	LOCAL	0.78	0.92	
MILK	LOCAL	0.56	0.72	
MILK	CO-OP	0.45	0.65	
EGGS	LOCAL	0.53	0.80	
EGGS	CO-OP	0.60	0.80	

In this example, you could insert a formula in the PROFIT field which would subtract the NET field from the RETAIL field and display the result. This formula would be something like '=RETAIL-NET'.

For You To Do

Find out how to add, subtract, multiply and divide fields in your database application and then try to recreate the example above.

1. Using the subtraction formula, calculate the PROFIT field. (The formula will look something like '=RETAIL-NET'.)
2. List all the produce supplied by the Co-op.
3. List all the produce supplied by local producers.
4. Save this database as RETAIL.

Assignment no. 37 The database shown below is used in a busy restaurant in town. It keeps track of the waitresses names, the tables they are serving, the price of the meal, and tips (if any). Create this database and carry out the instructions listed underneath.

TABLE	WAITRESS	COST(£)	TIPS(£)	TOTAL
1	CATHY	10.50	1.50	
2	EMMA	5.95	1.00	
3	CATHY	8.89	1.00	
4	JOANNE	5.67	0.00	
5	EMMA	7.89	0.50	
6	JOANNE	8.90	1.00	
7	CATHY	15.78	3.00	
8	MARY	4.50	0.00	
9	MARY	14.50	2.00	
10	JOANNE	9.78	2.00	
11	MARY	10.78	2.00	
12	EMMA	30.67	5.00	
13	CATHY	20.67	3.00	

1. Enter a formula in the TOTAL column which will calculate the total amount each customer paid for their meal.
2. Sort the records by WAITRESS.
3. Sort the records again, this time using the TIPS field.
4. Find out how many meals cost more than £8.00.
5. Print one copy of the database.
6. Save the database as MEAL.

Assignment no. 38

The local scouts are planning to go on three different trips this year. In preparation, they created a database to log the trips each scout was going on and how much money each would have to pay. The scouts can avail of all three options if they wish and the cost of each trip is given in the columns below.

NAME	CAMPING	HIKING	CANOEING	TOTAL
BURKE	80	25	30	
JONES	80	0	0	
BRENNAN	80	25	30	
MAGUIRE	80	0	30	
MITCHELL	80	25	0	
CAMPBELL	80	0	30	
SMITH	0	25	30	
O'BRIEN	0	25	30	
DOHERTY	80	25	0	
SWEENEY	80	0	0	

1. Find the total cost for each scout by entering an appropriate formula in the TOTAL field.
2. Search for scouts who are going on all three trips.
3. Search for scouts who are only going on the camping trip.
4. Search for scouts who are not going camping but are going hiking.
5. Sort the scouts in alphabetical order and print this list.
6. Save this database as SCOUT.

Assignment no. 39 The owner of a local paint shop has asked you to make a database of the items in stock. Define the field names, widths and datatypes and input the information as shown.

For You To Do

COLOUR	TYPE	RETAIL	AMOUNT_SOLD	TOTAL
WHITE	GLOSS	6.78	2	
WHITE	MATT	5.80	5	
WHITE	EMULSION	6.75	4	
BLACK	GLOSS	7.90	6	
BLACK	MATT	7.00	1	
BLACK	EMULSION	6.90	5	
RED	MATT	6.50	0	
RED	EMULSION	7.00	3	
RED	GLOSS	6.95	4	
BLUE	GLOSS	5.90	5	
BLUE	EMULSION	6.80	8	
BLUE	MATT	6.45	0	

1. Input a formula in the TOTAL field that calculates the total amount of money paid by customers. This should be based on the retail price and the amount sold.
2. Search for emulsion paints only.
3. Search for matt paints costing less than £6.70.
4. Search for emulsion paints costing £6.80 or more.
5. Sort the database according to paint colour.
6. Search the TOTAL field for amounts exceeding £40.00 and print the results of this search.
7. Save the database as PAINT.

More about Sorts

Up to now, all the sorts we've carried out on databases have been based on one field. It is possible though, to sort a database on more than one field. This is called multi-level sorting. Instead of having just one key field, two are used.

Multi-level Sorting

The *primary key field* is the first field to be sorted in the database.

The *secondary key field* is the second field to be sorted.

Example

NAME	AGE	SEX
JONES	16	M
MAGUIRE	14	F
SMITH	16	M
JONES	15	F
SMITH	15	F

If this database is sorted using the NAME field as the primary key field and the AGE field as the secondary key field, the computer will first sort the records using the NAME field and then sort the records using the AGE field. The result of this multi-level sort would be as follows.

NAME	AGE	SEX
JONES	15	F
JONES	16	M
MAGUIRE	14	F
SMITH	15	F
SMITH	16	M

As you can see, there are two Jones and two Smiths. The computer first sorted the database alphabetically by NAME, and then in ascending order by AGE.

> 1. Retrieve the database PAINT.
> 2. Sort the database using COLOUR as the primary key field and TYPE as the secondary key field.

For You To Do

Assignment no. 40 A newspaper stores all the TV schedules in a database and calls them up for printing when needed. Create the database below which is only a fraction of the real thing.

CHANNEL	TIME	PROGRAMME	COMMENTS
BBC 1	8.00	EASTENDERS	Cindy returns
BBC 1	9.00	NEWS	
RTE 1	8.00	HAMISH MACBETH	Hamish investigates a murder
NETWORK 2	8.00	BEVERLY HILLS 90210	More teenage stories
C4	7.00	NEWS	
C4	10.00	NYPD BLUE	Last in series
BBC 2	8.00	TOP GEAR	Results of survey
RTE 1	9.00	NEWS	
NETWORK 2	10.00	THE BILL	DS Greig gets away with murder
T na G	10.00	NUACHT	

1. Save this database as SCHEDULE.
2. Sort the database using CHANNEL as the primary key field and TIME as the secondary key field.
3. Search for programmes starting at 8.00 p.m.
4. Find out when the NEWS (or NUACHT) is on each channel.
5. Print one copy of the results of this search.

Assignment no. 41

The following information is typical of what you would find in a commercial database—in other words, people pay for information like this! The company you are working for needs to make a list of potential clients. Create this database and answer the questions below.

COMPANY	EMPLOYEES	TURNOVER	CONTACT	TEL
ACME FILMS	150	150,000,000	J. ADAMS	2356783
EUAN	50	50,000	E. ROBINSON	3356743
MICRO	27	47,000	S. FIRTH	3588765
WYR RADIO	44	120,000	A. DOHERTY	2477543
CEMENT LTD	67	300,000	G. GILL	3775322
CREDITBANK	266	2,670,800	M. RUSTOFF	3688743
NEWTECH	34	750,000	E. WEAFER	5466222
JUSTUS INC	45	800,000	M. BOYLAN	3775332
GRAFICK	22	589,000	P. JONES	2278564
SURFS	33	456,700	B. HAMMOND	3775432

1. Save this database as COMPANY.
2. Sort the database using the EMPLOYEES field as the primary key field and TURNOVER as the secondary key field.
3. Analysis of your sales figures has indicated that your best targets are companies with more than 40 employees and a turnover in excess of £500,000. Search for companies meeting these criteria and print out one copy of the results.
4. Now sort the database by COMPANY and print out one copy.

Assignment no. 42 A teacher has set up a database in order to store her students' test results. It lists each student's name, the tests they have done, the mark awarded in each test, and their average mark. Recreate this database as shown below.

NAME	CLASS	TEST1	TEST2	TEST3	TEST4	AVERAGE
S. JENNINGS	1A2	67	45	49	60	
A. GORMAN	1A1	56	59	65	70	
B. CAHILL	1A1	60	65	70	72	
C. CARBURY	1A3	70	75	74	80	
F. OWENS	1A4	68	70	74	80	
G. MITCHELL	1A2	80	87	80	87	
N. BRUTON	1A2	90	88	92	85	
M. KING	1A4	85	58	67	75	
F. LAMBERT	1A5	86	67	70	78	
Q. WINTHROP	1A6	67	70	63	72	

1. Save this database as MARKS.
2. Sort the database by CLASS.
3. Input a formula in the AVERAGE field that calculates the average mark of each student.
4. Sort the database using CLASS as the primary key field and AVERAGE as the secondary key field. Print out one copy of this sorted information.

A national bus company has decided to put all their route information, including distance, cost, etc., in to a database. Create this database, noting the field widths and datatypes, and carry out the instructions below.

Assignment no. 43

FROM	TO	DISTANCE	DEPART	ARRIVE
SLIGO	KILLARNEY	213	9.00	13.00
SLIGO	GALWAY	86	10.00	12.00
SLIGO	DUBLIN	135	11.00	14.30
GALWAY	DUBLIN	136	9.00	13.00
GALWAY	BELFAST	190	10.00	14.00
DUBLIN	CORK	160	9.00	12.30
DUBLIN	BELFAST	105	9.00	11.30
DUBLIN	LIMERICK	125	10.00	13.00
DERRY	SLIGO	85	9.00	10.45
DERRY	BELFAST	70	9.00	11.00

1. Save the database as ROUTES.
2. Sort the database using the FROM field as the primary key field and DISTANCE as the secondary key field.
3. The fare for each journey is calculated on a per mile basis: 1 mile = £0.08. Add a new field called FARE and enter a formula that will calculate the fare for each journey.
4. Print out one copy of the database.

Enhancements

It is quite easy to enhance the layout or look of a database. For example, making a particular field bold or italic will make the information contained in that field stand out. There are other style changes that can be applied too, such as centring text within a field or changing the colour of text. The format of a Data Entry Form can also be enhanced so that the person inputting the information is presented with an easy-to-read form. Look at the examples shown below.

Example 1

NAME	ADDRESS	AGE	SEX
J. SMITH	1 THE GABLES	22	*F*
A. BOLTON	23 OLD ROAD	34	*M*
C. DONOVAN	17 MAIN ST	28	*F*

In Example 1, the NAME field has been emboldened (made bold), a different font has been used for the ADDRESS and AGE fields, and the SEX field has been italicized (made italic). You could also choose to use a different colour for a particular field.

Example 2

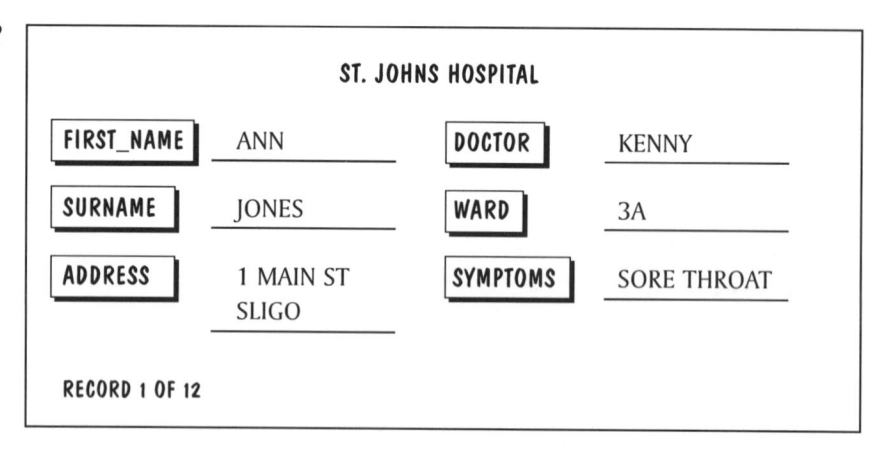

```
                    ST. JOHNS HOSPITAL

   ┌───────────┐                    ┌──────────┐
   │FIRST_NAME │   ANN              │ DOCTOR   │   KENNY
   └───────────┘  ─────────         └──────────┘  ─────────

   ┌───────────┐                    ┌──────────┐
   │ SURNAME   │   JONES            │  WARD    │   3A
   └───────────┘  ─────────         └──────────┘  ─────────

   ┌───────────┐                    ┌──────────┐
   │ ADDRESS   │   1 MAIN ST        │ SYMPTOMS │   SORE THROAT
   └───────────┘   SLIGO            └──────────┘  ─────────

   RECORD 1 OF 12
```

Example 2 shows a data entry form. The fields have been enhanced by adding a box or border with a shadow, and by choosing a nice font. It is important to leave enough space for a field like SYMPTOMS, which could contain a lot of text.

You can easily see the difference between these two examples. The first layout lists all the records in the database. It is usually easier to use this method when dealing with queries as it allows query results to be listed clearly on screen. The second layout (the Data Entry Form) is also commonly used, but it does have one major disadvantage—only one record can be viewed at a time. On the plus side, data input is generally easier with a Data Entry Form.

Remember, when enhancing a database don't go overboard—keep it simple. Any enhancements should improve the look of the database, not distract the user.

Assignment no. 44

In this assignment, you must use a data entry form to input the information given below in to a database. You can enhance it as you see fit. The information has been taken from the results of a questionnaire which a group of Transition Year students carried out within the school.

NUMBER refers to the number of respondents per class, POCKET MONEY refers to the average amount of pocket money per week, and HOMEWORK refers to the average number of hours spent doing homework per day.

CLASS	NUMBER	POCKET MONEY	HOMEWORK	TOTAL_HOMEWORK
1A1	20	5.60	2.00	
1A2	23	6.00	2.50	
1A3	21	5.70	2.00	
1A4	24	5.23	1.50	
1A5	18	5.34	2.50	
1A6	17	5.45	2.00	
2A1	19	6.10	2.50	
2A2	23	6.50	1.50	
2A3	21	6.20	2.25	
2A4	22	5.90	2.45	
2A5	20	6.50	2.50	

1. Save the database as QUEST.
2. Sort the database using the CLASS field as the primary key field.
3. Enter a formula in the TOTAL_HOMEWORK field to work out the total number of hours each class spends doing homework.
4. Insert a new field called TOTAL_MONEY. Input a formula in to this field that will work out the total amount of pocket money each class receives each week.
5. Sort the database according to this field (TOTAL_MONEY).
6. Print out one copy of the results.

Indexing

We have all seen indexes before. An index at the beginning of a book is simply a page showing where each section or chapter of the book is located. The index is normally quite short compared to the book itself—it's usually only a few pages long.

In the same way, an index can be created for a database. A database index is a very small file which holds information about the position of the records in the database.

Why Use an Index? You may have noticed that when a new record is added to a database just after a sort has been done, the database has to be re-sorted again because the new record is not in the correct position. When you index a database, the index automatically updates the database and puts the record in the correct position. Most database users prefer to index a database rather than re-sort it each time a new record is added.

Example

RECORD NO.	PRODUCT	PRICE	IN_STOCK
1	TEA BAGS	1.60	Y
2	SUGAR	0.84	N
3	BUTTER	0.75	Y
4	MILK	0.50	Y
5	BREAD	0.64	N

This is an unsorted database. It will now be sorted using the PRICE field.

RECORD NO.	PRODUCT	PRICE	IN_STOCK
4	MILK	0.50	Y
5	BREAD	0.64	N
3	BUTTER	0.75	Y
2	SUGAR	0.84	N
1	TEA BAGS	1.60	Y

The records have been sorted according to PRICE. Note how their positions have changed.

RECORD NO.
4
5
3
2
1

This is the indexed file. Take note that it doesn't contain the records themselves, only the position of the records within the database. Record number 4 is first while record number 1 is last.

If we added a new record to this database, the index would update itself automatically. Indexing is another way of sorting records. It is permanent and can take account of changes without the user needing to re-sort the database.

Assignment no. 45

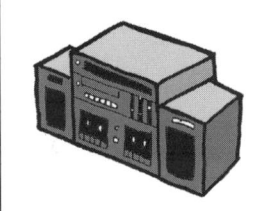

In this assignment you must create the database shown below, index it, and then add some new records. This is a database of your music collection. It contains the name of the artist, the name of the album, where the album was bought, etc. After indexing, you should see the database update itself automatically when you add new records.

ARTIST	ALBUM	BOUGHT	DATE
MEATLOAF	BAT OUT OF HELL	HMV	13/04/95
MICHAEL JACKSON	HISTORY	GOLDEN DISCS	04/06/97
DAVID BOWIE	BEST OF	LOCAL	19/03/94
U2	POP	HMV	23/08/97
PRODIGY	FAT OF THE LAND	GOLDEN DISCS	21/05/97
OASIS	THIS BE NOW	LOCAL	13/09/97
SIMPLY RED	STARS	VIRGIN	12/07/97
U2	JOSHUA TREE	HMV	13/06/97
OASIS	WHAT'S THE STORY	LOCAL	23/06/96
SPICE GIRLS	SPICE	VIRGIN	13/08/97

1. Save this database as MUSIC1.
2. Insert a new field called CD/TAPE and indicate whether the album is a CD or a tape. (Make up this information yourself.)
3. Create an index using the ARTIST field.
4. Add the following records to your database:

ARTIST	ALBUM	BOUGHT	DATE	CD/TAPE
ABBA	GOLD	HMV	13/04/96	CD
HOT CHOCOLATE	GREATEST HITS	GOLDEN DISCS	17/06/97	CD
DANIEL O'DONNELL	BEST OF	LOCAL	23/03/97	TAPE

5. Search for albums bought before 23/03/97.
6. Enhance the database as you see fit.
7. Search for all albums purchased locally.
8. Save the updated database as MUSIC2.

Assignment no. 46 Create the following database. Define the field names, widths and datatypes, and input the data given below.

PLAYER	TEAM	NATIONALITY	WORTH(£m)
IRWIN	MAN UTD	IRISH	3.5
ADAMS	ARSENAL	ENGLISH	4
BABB	LIVERPOOL	IRISH	3
KEANE	MAN UTD	IRISH	6
SHEARER	NEWCASTLE	ENGLISH	15
SUTTON	BLACKBURN	ENGLISH	5
STAUNTON	ASTON VILLA	IRISH	4
INCE	LIVERPOOL	ENGLISH	6

1. Save this database as FOOTBALL.
2. Create an index using the PLAYER field.
3. Add your own record!
4. Enhance the database as you see fit.
5. Search for players worth more than £4 million.
6. Search for Irish players worth more than £4 million.
7. Find all the Manchester United players that are Irish.
8. Search for Irish players who play for either Liverpool or Manchester United.
9. Print out the complete database.

Assignment no. 47

Here's another database for you to create! In this assignment you are working in the Natural History Museum, making a database for the public on dinosaurs! This database will contain information on dinosaur names, their meaning, the era during which the dinosaurs existed, the year their remains were discovered, their weight, and the foods they ate.

NAME	MEANING	ERA	FOUND	WEIGHT	FOOD
TYRANNOSAURUS	Tyrant Lizard	Cretaceous	1902	6.4 tonnes	Dinosaurs
BARYONYX	Heavy Claw	Cretaceous	1983	2.0 tonnes	Fish, dead animals
DILOPHOSAURUS	Two-ridge Lizard	Jurassic	1942	500 kg	Dinosaurs
OVIRAPTOR	Egg Thief	Cretaceous	1923	33 kg	Eggs
KENTROSAURUS	Spiky Lizard	Jurassic	1900	1 tonne	Plants
IGUANODON	Iguana Tooth	Cretaceous	1825	4.5 tonnes	Plants
TRICERATOPS	Three-horned Face	Cretaceous	1880	5.5 tonnes	Plants
CETIOSAURUS	Whale Lizard	Jurassic	1869	27 tonnes	Plants
CARNOTAURUS	Carnivorous Bull	Cretaceous	1985	1 tonne	Dinosaurs
ANCHISAURUS	Near Lizard	Jurassic	1912	27 kg	Plants

1. Save this database as DINOSAUR.
2. Insert a new field called LENGTH. The length (in feet) of each dinosaur is as follows (from Tyrannosaurus down to Anchisaurus): 39, 34, 19, 7, 16, 30, 29, 59, 25, 8.
3. Create an index using the LENGTH field.
4. Search for dinosaurs from the Jurassic period.
5. Search for plant-eating dinosaurs from the Jurassic period.
6. Print out one copy of this search.
7. Search for dinosaurs that were cannibals!

Assignment no. 48 A turf accountant (or bookie!) has decided to use a database to hold information on all the horses running in a particular race. He is entering the following details for each horse: the name of the horse, its form (form refers to the position of the horse in the last five races), the number of days since the horse last ran, its trainer, the age of the horse, and how much weight it's carrying. Create this database using the information below.

NAME	FORM	LAST_RAN	TRAINER	AGE	WEIGHT
BLUE STEEL	42212	31	J. THOMSON	5	9 1
LIGHTNING	13328	40	E. MACKEY	3	8 12
PROJECT X	00300	8	H. KENNEDY	5	8 9
SPEED MACHINE	01002	8	L. ROGERS	5	8 12
EL DORADO	00050	12	C. MURPHY	4	9
RED ROSE	00203	14	O. WHENT	3	8 6
HIDDEN AGENDA	10201	22	B. SMITH	5	8 6
STORM RIDER	01103	48	D. CALLUM	5	9 2
WHITE DANCER	65220	23	N. NUGENT	3	9
EASY MONEY	30225	19	J. BROWN	4	8 12

1. Save the database as RACE.
2. Create an index using the FORM field.
3. Add the following late entries:

NAME	FORM	LAST_RAN	TRAINER	AGE	WEIGHT
THE ENFORCER	00321	12	J. OLWELL	4	8 8
FANCY THAT	11021	19	C. KENT	3	9

4. Search for horses that ran a race within the last 20 days.
5. Search for horses carrying a weight of more that 8 8.
6. Print out the complete database.

A mini-company in your school has decided to sell gemstones. A database containing reference information on common gemstones needs to be created (see below). This is your job! The fields in this database should contain the name of the gemstone, the month for which it is a birthstone, its meaning as a birthstone (i.e., what it symbolises), its colour, and the minerals it contains.

Assignment no. 49

GEMSTONE	MONTH	MEANING	COLOUR	MINERALS
GARNET	JANUARY	FAITHFULNESS	DEEP RED	calcium, magnesium, iron, titanium
AMETHYST	FEBRUARY	SINCERITY	VIOLET	quartz
AQUAMARINE	MARCH	COURAGE	BLUE/GREEN	beryllium, aluminium
DIAMOND	APRIL	INNOCENCE	COLOURLESS	carbon
EMERALD	MAY	LOVE	GREEN	beryllium
PEARL	JUNE	CONTENTMENT	WHITE	-
RUBY	JULY	HAPPINESS	RED	corundum
PERIDOT	AUGUST	HAPPY MARRIAGE	GREEN	olivine
SAPPHIRE	SEPTEMBER	CLEAR THOUGHT	DEEP BLUE	corundum
OPAL	OCTOBER	HOPE	BLACK, VARIETY	quartz

1. Save the database as GEM.
2. Create an index using the MONTH field.
3. Add the following records:

GEMSTONE	MONTH	MEANING	COLOUR	MINERALS
TOPAZ	NOVEMBER	FIDELITY	YELLOW/BROWN	aluminium, fluorine
TURQUOISE	DECEMBER	PROSPERITY	BLUE	copper, aluminium phosphate

4. Search for gemstones containing aluminium.
5. Print out the results of that search.
6. Search for gemstones that are green.

Assignment no. 50 This database contains information about the Beaufort scale of wind forces. The database lists the force number (0–12), a description of the wind, the effects and the speed of the wind (m.p.h.). Create the database as shown and carry out the instructions below.

FORCE_NO	DESCRIPTION	EFFECT	SPEED
0	CALM	Smoke rises straight up	1
1	LIGHT AIR	Smoke shows wind direction	3
2	LIGHT BREEZE	Feel wind on face	7
3	GENTLE BREEZE	Leaves move	12
4	MODERATE BREEZE	Small branches move	18
5	FRESH BREEZE	Small trees sway	24
6	STRONG BREEZE	Telegraph wires whistle	31
7	MODERATE GALE	Difficult to walk against wind	38
8	FRESH GALE	Twigs break	46
9	STRONG GALE	Slates blow off roofs	54

1. Save this database as BEAUFORT.
2. Create an index using the FORCE field.
3. Add the following records:

FORCE_NO	DESCRIPTION	EFFECT	SPEED
10	FULL GALE	Trees uprooted	63
11	STORM	Widespread destruction	75
12	HURRICANE	Towns flattened	>75

4. Search for winds greater than 30 m.p.h.
5. Print out the complete database.
6. Search for effects that contain the word 'wind'.
7. What effects can you expect when the wind speed is between 50 and 65 m.p.h.?

A career guidance teacher would like to have the points requirements for some third-level courses entered in to a database. The information is given below. Create the database as shown and answer the questions that follow.

Assignment no. 51

For You To Do

CODE	COURSE	LEVEL	COLLEGE	POINTS
DN008	Science	Degree	UCD	410
DN012	Arts	Degree	UCD	380
DN009	Law	Degree	UCD	490
DN002	Medicine	Degree	UCD	575
GY009	Science	Degree	UCG	385
CK102	Social Science	Degree	UCC	425
TR072	Pharmacy	Degree	TCD	545
DC111	Business Studies	Degree	DCU	420
LY012	Computer Science	Cert./Diploma	Letterkenny RTC	200
FT353	Journalism	Degree	DIT	450
LM021	Language/Computing	Degree	UL	455
CW008	Construction Studies	Cert./Diploma	Carlow RTC	200

1. Save this database as POINTS.
2. Select a suitable field to create an index.
3. Enhance the database as you see fit.
4. Search for courses in UCD requiring less than 430 points.
5. Search for courses in RTCs only.
6. Print the results of this search.
7. Add the following records:

CODE	COURSE	LEVEL	COLLEGE	POINTS
SG135	Applied Tourism	Cert./Diploma	Sligo RTC	310
CK101	Arts	Degree	UCC	385

8. Create a new index using another suitable field.
9. Search for courses in Cork requiring less than 500 points.

Assignment no. 52
Part 1

It is possible to copy records from one database to another and in this assignment you will learn how to do this. We will be working with GAA football information. (This assignment is quite long and can be carried out in stages if time is against you.)

In the first instance, you must create a separate database for each province listing the following: the counties taking part, their team colours, the province, and the last time they won the Sam Maguire Cup (if ever!). Make the four separate databases and save each one as the name of the province.

COUNTY	PROVINCE	COLOURS	YEAR_WON
DONEGAL	ULSTER	yellow, green	1992
DOWN	ULSTER	red, black	1994
MONAGHAN	ULSTER	white, blue	-
ANTRIM	ULSTER	yellow, white	-
CAVAN	ULSTER	blue, white	1952
DERRY	ULSTER	red, white	1993
ARMAGH	ULSTER	orange, white	-
TYRONE	ULSTER	white, red	-
FERMANAGH	ULSTER	green, white	-

COUNTY	PROVINCE	COLOURS	YEAR_WON
KILKENNY	LEINSTER	yellow, black	-
DUBLIN	LEINSTER	blue, navy	1995
OFFALY	LEINSTER	yellow, white, green	1982
MEATH	LEINSTER	yellow, green	1996
CARLOW	LEINSTER	red, yellow, green	-
WESTMEATH	LEINSTER	maroon, white	-
LONGFORD	LEINSTER	blue, yellow	-
LAOIS	LEINSTER	blue, white	-
WEXFORD	LEINSTER	purple, yellow	1918
KILDARE	LEINSTER	white	1928
WICKLOW	LEINSTER	blue, yellow	-
LOUTH	LEINSTER	red, white	1957

Here is the information for the final two databases. Note how all four databases have identical field names and their fields are in the same order. This will make it very easy for us later on when we want to copy records from one database to another.

**Assignment no. 52
Part 2**

For You To Do

COUNTY	PROVINCE	COLOURS	YEAR_WON
MAYO	CONNACHT	green, red	1951
GALWAY	CONNACHT	maroon, white	1966
LONDON	CONNACHT	green, white	-
SLIGO	CONNACHT	black, white	-
ROSCOMMON	CONNACHT	yellow, blue	1944
LEITRIM	CONNACHT	yellow, green	-

COUNTY	PROVINCE	COLOURS	YEAR_WON
CLARE	MUNSTER	yellow, blue	-
CORK	MUNSTER	red, white	1990
KERRY	MUNSTER	green, yellow	1997
WATERFORD	MUNSTER	white, blue	-
TIPPERARY	MUNSTER	blue, yellow	1920
LIMERICK	MUNSTER	green, white	1896

1. After all that work, you must now create and save a new database called SAM using the same design as above.
2. Select and copy all the records from each of the province databases and paste them in to the new database.
3. Create an index using the COUNTY field.
4. Search for counties with red on their shirts.
5. Search for counties that have never won the championship.
6. Print out a copy of all the counties that have won the championship.
7. Compile a list of those counties that have won the championship since 1990.
8. Search for counties with green in their shirts who have won the championship.
9. Sort the database using a suitable field and print out one complete copy of it.

Assessment Log Book

TASK	METHOD	DATE/SIGNATURE
Understand the concept of a database	Oral, Written Test	
Understand fields and records	Oral, Written Test	
Field width	Oral, Assignment No. 28	
Field datatypes	Assignment No. 28	
Saving and editing	Assignment No. 28	
Adding records	Assignment No. 29	
Searching records	Assignment No. 30	
Printing	Assignment No. 31	
Sorting and the key field	Assignment Nos. 32, 33, 34, 35	
Adding and deleting fields	Assignment No. 36	
Using mathematics on fields	Assignment Nos. 37, 38, 39	
Multi-level sorting; primary and secondary key fields	Assignment Nos. 40, 41, 42, 43	
Enhancements	Assignment No. 44	
Indexing	Assignment Nos. 45–51	
Copying between databases	Assignment No. 52	

PART IV SPREADSHEETS

Introduction

Before computers were as widely used as they are today, people had to do their sums and calculations by hand—either writing the calculations on a piece of paper or on a blackboard. If a lot of numbers were involved, mistakes could easily be made. Take the following example:

MONTH	JAN	FEB	MAR	APR	MAY	JUN
SAVINGS	0	290	585	876	1223	1615
CAR LOAN	120	120	120	120	120	120
RENT	350	350	350	350	350	350
FOOD	200	195	210	220	180	187
ESB	60	65	59	63	68	56
OIL	80	75	70	50	40	30
TOTAL	810	805	809	803	758	743
SALARY	1100	1100	1100	1150	1150	1150
SURPLUS	290	295	291	347	392	407

Let's look at the first month only. This person has no savings coming in to January as Christmas cleaned him out! Adding up all his expenses for January—car loan, food, etc.—he has outgoings of £810. His salary for the month is £1100, leaving him with a surplus of £290 going in to February. Because figures from one month are carried over to the next month, a single mistake in the calculations would have caused the whole exercise to be a waste of time. We would have to start our calculations from scratch again. This example only shows the first half of the year—just imagine the work involved if a mistake was discovered when twelve months of the year had been calculated!

Spreadsheets are computer programmes that can help avoid difficulties like these. The beauty of a spreadsheet is that it does all the calculating for you. So even if you make a mistake, all you have to do is correct it and the computer will automatically recalculate your figures.

> Find out the name of the spreadsheet application you are using in school. Most spreadsheets have the same features and a similar design. We will now look at what you can expect to see when you open up a spreadsheet.

For You To Do

Screen Layout

When you enter a spreadsheet application for the first time, you should see a screen with columns and rows. Each column is given a letter and each row a number. Where a column intersects a row you have a *cell* (it's the little box).

Cell Address

Each cell in a spreadsheet has an address. This address is determined by the column and the row in which the cell is located. The cells B2 and D4 are shown below.

What cell is the number 45 in?
What is contained in D1?

When you go into a spreadsheet, you only see a small part of the complete sheet. It can contain thousands of cells. The part you are looking at is a small 'window' of the complete sheet.

	A	B	C	D
1				90
2		cell B2		
3				
4		45		cell D4
5				

Cell Attributes

Cells normally contain one of three things: a value, a label or a formula.

Value A value is any number that can be calculated, e.g., 1, 100, 1000, etc. Dates and times cannot be calculated.

Label A label is simply text, e.g., END OF YEAR PROFIT.

Formula Formulae are simple to use. The same symbols are used in spreadsheets as are used in mathematics:

+ add
- subtract
* multiply
/ divide

When using formulae in a spreadsheet, cell addresses are referred to, not the actual values contained within the cells. For example, we could enter the formula '=C2+C3+C4' and this will add everything in the cells C2, C3 and C4. In this way, if you change a value in a cell, you don't have to change the formula.

Now, let's see why the cell address is entered in a formula and not the value within the cell itself.

Example

	A	B	C	D
1				
2		10		
3		20		
4		20		
5		B2+B3+B4		

In this spreadsheet, there are three values in cells B2, B3 and B4. There is a simple addition formula assigned to B5 and the result of this addition formula will appear here (50). If you change the value in B2 from 10 to 30, the answer in B5 will automatically change as well! This is because we are adding the values in the three cell addresses.

If, however, you apply the formula '+10+20+20' to cell B5, the number 50 will also appear here. Changing the value in B2 from 10 to 30 would have no effect on the value in B5. This is because the computer is adding the values 10, 20 and 20, not B2+B3+B4.

Normally, you don't see a formula in a cell, only the result of the formula.

Study the spreadsheet below and work out the formulae required for the TOTAL column and the REMAINDER row.

For You To Do

	A	B	C	D	E
1		JAN	FEB	MAR	TOTAL
2	SALES	200	300	400	
3	EXPENSES	100	150	300	
4	REMAINDER				
5					

1. When you have worked out what formulae to use, try creating this spreadsheet on your computer.
2. Save this spreadsheet as SALES.
3. Change the value in B2 to 140 and change D3 to 290. Did the computer automatically recalculate for you?

Assignment no. 53 Your first spreadsheet assignment is very easy. All you have to do is copy this spreadsheet—the formulae you need have even been given! A shopkeeper wants to use the spreadsheet to calculate the retail price of some of the goods in his shop. He will multiply the net price by the VAT rate (21%) to get the RETAIL price.

For You To Do

	A	B	C	D
1	ITEM	NET	RETAIL	TOTAL
2	SOAP	0.78	B2*21%	B2+C2
3	TOOTHPASTE	1.24	B3*21%	B3+C3
4	BEANS	0.30	B4*21%	B4+C4
5	BREAD	0.68	B5*21%	B5+C5
6	MILK	0.54	B6*21%	B6+C6
7	PEAS	0.29	B7*21%	B7+C7
8	BURGERS	1.80	B8*21%	B8+C8
9	JAM	0.90	B9*21%	B9+C9
10	MAYONNAISE	1.45	B10*21%	B10+C10

1. Save this spreadsheet as SHOP.
2. Make the following changes:
   - Beans have increased in price by £0.05
   - Bread has decreased in price by £0.02
   - Burgers are now £1.95
3. Change the VAT rate on toothpaste to 30%.
4. In cell E1, type DISCOUNT. The shopkeeper is offering a discount on all the goods in the shop. This discount is 25%. In cell E2, insert the formula D2/4. In cell F1, type the heading NEWPRICE. In cell F2, insert a formula to subtract the discount from the old price.
5. Save your file again and print out one copy of the completed spreadsheet.

Enhancements

If you have already studied word processing, you will be familiar with enhancing text and numbers. Similar enhancements can be applied to spreadsheets. You can use different fonts, different styles (bold, italic and underline) and different justification (centre, left or right justification). You can also use different colours to enhance the look of your work.

Apart from aligning the text and numbers in a spreadsheet, it is also very easy to get the computer to add in decimal points, £ signs, % signs, etc. This is called FORMATTING the numbers. Take the following examples:

	A	B	C	D	E	F
1		JAN	FEB	MAR	APR	TOTAL
2	RENT	400	400	400	400	
3	CAR	120	125	120	115	
4	BILLS	60	65	55	55	
5	FOOD	190	210	230	220	

Before formatting

	A	B	C	D	E	F
1		JAN	FEB	MAR	APR	TOTAL
2	RENT	£400.00	£400.00	£400.00	£400.00	
3	CAR	£120.00	£125.00	£120.00	£115.00	
4	BILLS	£60.00	£65.00	£55.00	£55.00	
5	FOOD	£190.00	£210.00	£230.00	£220.00	

After formatting

For You To Do

As you can see, formatting makes a huge difference to the look of the spreadsheet. Try creating the spreadsheet above and input the relevant formulae yourself.

1. Save the spreadsheet as RENT.
2. Enhance it by using a different font for the months.
3. Format the numbers as currency values to two decimal places (as shown in the example above).
4. Save again and print out one copy of the completed spreadsheet.

Assignment no. 54 In this assignment, you are asked to input the information below in to a spreadsheet. You should input the relevant formulae and enhance the spreadsheet according to the instructions given.

	A	B	C	D	E
1					
2	COUNTRY	CURRENCY	BANK BUYS	BANK SELLS	DIFFERENCE
3	UK	Sterling	0.9170	0.8730	
4	US	Dollar	1.5485	1.4805	
5	Canada	Can. Dlr.	2.1190	2.0390	
6	Australia	Aus. Dlr.	2.0975	2.00	
7	Austria	Aus. Sch.	19.4110	18.41	
8	Belgium	B. Franc	56.4500	53.45	
9	Denmark	D. Krone	10.5000	9.95	
10	Finland	F. Markaa	8.1675	7.54	
11	France	Fr. Franc	9.3485	8.89	
12	Germany	D-mark	2.7630	2.6230	
13	Greece	Gr. Drachma	432.00	407.00	
14	Holland	Guilder	3.1080	2.94	

1. Save this spreadsheet as CURRENCY.
2. Format the currency values to four decimal places.
3. Make the 'Country' column bold and change the font.
4. Make the headings italic (row 2).
5. Input a formula in column E to calculate the difference between the buying and selling prices of the bank.
6. Change column B to bold (the 'Currency' column).
7. Insert the heading 'Bureau de Change' in cell A1.
8. Save these changes and print out one copy of the complete spreadsheet.

This spreadsheet could easily be used by a car rental company to calculate the hire price of a car. All the cars have been categorised in groups according to their engine size. The hire price of a car is determined by two factors: the number of days the car is required for and the group to which it belongs (e.g., a 1.1 litre car will be cheaper to hire than a 2.0 litre car).

Assignment no. 55

For You To Do

	A	B	C	D
1	CAR HIRE			
2				Price/Day
3			Group A	£25
4			Group B	£30
5			Group C	£35
6			Group D	£40
7			Group E	£45
8	Customer Name	Group	No. of Days	Cost
9	Adams	A	10	D3*C9
10	Wilson	B	7	
11	Boylan	C	8	
12	Jones	E	12	
13	Macari	E	10	
14	Peters	C	2	

The first formula needed is shown in cell D9—the cost of a group A car (per day) multiplied by the number of days the car is being hired for.

1. Input formulae for the remaining cells in column D.
2. Wilson (row 10) has decided to take the car for another day. How much will her car hire bill be now?
3. The price of cars in groups D and E has increased by £5 per day. Make the necessary changes.
4. Save the spreadsheet as HIRE and print out one copy.

Sum and Range

Look carefully at the following sample spreadsheet. This is a fairly straightforward budget created for the year. You can see that the TOTAL row (row 14) requires 12 cells of information (Jan–Dec) to be added for each of the columns.

	A	B	C	D	E	F
1		RENT	ESB	HEATING	FOOD	TOTAL
2	JAN	200	50	60	200	
3	FEB	200	48	60	210	
4	MAR	200	45	58	230	
5	APR	200	46	55	190	
6	MAY	200	47	50	205	
7	JUNE	200	38	40	210	
8	JUL	200	35	20	220	
9	AUG	200	49	20	200	
10	SEP	200	42	20	205	
11	OCT	200	41	35	210	
12	NOV	200	46	50	220	
13	DEC	200	50	50	250	
14	TOTAL					

If you wanted to find the total amount spent on heating for the year, you could use the formula 'D2+D3+D4+D5+D6+D7+D8+D9+D10+D11+D12+D13'. Apart from being very messy and bulky, it is also very easy to make a mistake with a formula this long. Wouldn't it be a better idea to specify the first and last cells and tell the computer to add everything in between? This is exactly what a *range* does.

In the spreadsheet shown above, you could use a formula like 'SUM(D2:D13)'. SUM means 'add'. Read this formula as: 'add everything between D2 and D13 inclusive'. [The spreadsheet package you are using may be slightly different.] The formula for the total amount spent in January would be 'SUM(B2:E2)'. In other words, 'add everything between B2 and E2 inclusive'.

For You To Do

1. Create the spreadsheet shown above. (You need only input the first six months if you haven't time to complete the entire spreadsheet.)
2. Enter the appropriate formulae in the TOTAL cells using the SUM and range functions discussed.
3. Save the spreadsheet as RANGE and print out one copy.

A hotel uses a number of different spreadsheets. This one is used for calculating the cost of foodstuffs used in the kitchen. It deals only with vegetables and meat. The prices shown are the amounts paid by the hotel for each item per week.

Assignment no. 56

For You To Do

	A	B	C	D	E	F
1	KITCHEN					
2		Week 1	Week 2	Week 3	Week 4	TOTAL
3	VEGETABLES					
4	Potatoes	£80	£75	£78	£82	
5	Carrots	£12	£10	£11	£15	
6	Beans	£8	£12	£11	£9	
7	Broccoli	£10	£11	£15	£13	
8						
9	MEAT					
10	Fillet Steak	£250	£200	£180	£190	
11	T-Bone Steak	£190	£210	£170	£180	
12	Sirloin Steak	£170	£150	£155	£140	
13						
14	TOTAL					

1. Create this spreadsheet and input formulae using the SUM and range functions to calculate the totals for column F and row 14.
2. Format the prices to two decimal places.
3. Enhance the spreadsheet by making the headings in row 2 italic. Make cells F2 and A14 bold.
4. Change the data in A6 to parsnips.
5. Change the data in D7 to £14.
6. Save this spreadsheet as KITCHEN and print out one copy.

Assignment no. 57 This spreadsheet is an example of an invoice. It describes the goods sold, the quantity and unit price for each item delivered. Column E will contain a formula to calculate the price for each item.

For You To Do

	A	B	C	D	E
1	OFFICE SUPPLIES	INVOICE			
2					
3	DESCRIPTION	QUANTITY	UNIT PRICE		COST
4	2-pin adapter	1	£2.56		
5	power cable	3	£4.56		
6	filing cabinet	1	£89.67		
7	keyboard	4	£21.78		
8	mouse	6	£9.67		
9	mouse mat	3	£2.99		
10	CD rack	2	£12.67		
11	desk tidy	3	£5.69		
12				SUBTOTAL	
13				VAT@21%	
14				TOTAL	

1. Input the data shown above, enhancing the spreadsheet as you see fit.
2. Insert formulae in Column E to calculate the cost of each item (multiply the unit price by the quantity sold).
3. Insert a formula in cell E12 to determine the SUBTOTAL (i.e., before tax is added).
4. Insert a formula in cell E13 to calculate the total amount of VAT payable (multiply the subtotal by 21%).
5. Calculate the total cost.
6. Save the spreadsheet as INVOICE and print out one copy.

Copying Formulae

Most spreadsheet packages have a facility that allows you to copy formulae from one row to another or from one column to another. Look at the following example.

	A	B	C	D	E
1	SALES '98				
2	Salesperson	Region A	Region B	Region C	Total
3	Jones	1200	1300	1400	SUM(B3:D3)
4	Murphy	1250	1350	1300	SUM(B4:D4)
5	Reynolds	1300	1200	1400	SUM(B5:D5)
6	TOTAL	SUM(B3:B5)	SUM(C3:C5)	SUM(D3:D5)	
7					

Let's look at the formulae in column E first. The only difference between the formulae in this column is the row number referred to. The computer can easily change the row numbers in a formula as you copy it down through the rows.

In row 6, the formulae differ only in the column letter referred to. It is quite straightforward for the computer to replace the column letters as the formula is being copied across.

This type of copying is called *relative copying*. The formula in each row or column is relative to the other rows or columns. (A touch of Einstein here!)

Relative Copying

For You To Do

1. Find out how to copy formulae in your spreadsheet package and then create the spreadsheet shown above.
2. Insert a formula in cell E3 to calculate the total for Jones.
3. Copy this formula and apply it to the other salespeople.
4. Insert a formula in cell B6 to calculate the total for Region A.
5. Copy this formula across the other regions.
6. Enhance the spreadsheet as you see fit.
7. Save this spreadsheet as SALES and print out one copy.

Assignment no. 58 A builder has been contracted to build a house and must provide his clients with a price estimate. Create the following spreadsheet which will enable him to determine the cost of the house. It takes into account the cost of supplies and labour. This type of spreadsheet could be used repeatedly by simply changing the supplies and/or labour requirements.

For You To Do

	A	B	C	D	E
1					
2	Supplies		Unit Cost	Number	Total
3		Wood	7.90	20	C3*D3
4		Brick	0.75	400	
5		Cement	8.90	4	
6		Plasterboard	15.78	10	
7					
8	Labour		Cost/Hour	No. of Hours	Total
9		Labourer	9.00	40	
10		Bricklayer	15.00	40	
11		Plasterer	15.00	20	
12				Subtotal	
13				VAT@21%	
14				TOTAL	

1. The formula given in E3 calculates the cost of wood. Copy this formula and apply it to the other supplies.
2. A similar formula is required to work out labour costs. Insert an appropriate formula to calculate the cost of a labourer and copy this formula for the other workers.
3. The SUBTOTAL is the cost of all the labour and supplies before VAT. Insert a SUM function in cell E12 to calculate this.
4. VAT is at a rate of 21%. Insert a formula in cell E13 to calculate the VAT for this contract (multiply the subtotal by 21%).
5. Calculate the TOTAL cost of the project.
6. Enhance the spreadsheet as you see fit.
7. Save as BUILDER.
8. Print out one copy of the completed spreadsheet.

A company buys several items each month for use in their manufacturing process. The price of these items fluctuates all the time, going up and down depending on various economic factors. Create the spreadsheet shown below which details the company's buying records for the first six months of the year.

Assignment no. 59

For You To Do

	A	B	C	D	E	F	G	H
1	ACME TRADING							
2								
3	Month	Jan	Feb	Mar	Apr	May	Jun	TOTAL
4								
5	No. of items	22	24	22	20	25	23	
6	Cost per item	£4	£4.25	£4.30	£4.15	£4.23	£4.18	
7	Total Cost							
8	Discount (20%)							
9	Net Cost							
10								

1. Carry out the following two enhancements:
   - Make the months bold and right justified;
   - Centre the heading in column A and put it in italics.
2. Insert a formula in cell B7 to calculate the total cost of the items for January.
3. Copy this formula to the other months in this row.
4. In cell B8, insert a formula to calculate a discount of 20%. [Hint: It will probably look like B7*20/100.]
5. Copy this formula to the other months in this row.
6. In cell B9, insert a formula that works out the net cost of the items, i.e., the total cost minus the discount.
7. Copy this formula to the other months in this row.
8. In cell H7, insert a formula to calculate the total cost of items for the six-month period.
9. Save the completed spreadsheet as ACME and print out a copy.

Average, Maximum and Minimum

Most spreadsheets have a host of functions available but we will only concern ourselves with the three most common: *average*, *maximum* and *minimum*. The following example illustrates how these functions work.

	A	B	C	D	E	F
1	SCORES					
2		Test 1	Test 2	Test 3	Average	Maximum
3	Jones	56	60	65	average(B3:D3)	maximum(B3:D3)
4	Waters	60	65	65	average(B4:D4)	maximum(B4:D4)
5	Martin	70	78	80	average(B5:D5)	maximum(B5:D5)
6	Reilly	78	74	70	average(B6:D6)	maximum(B6:D6)
7	Lennon	70	90	80	average(B7:D7)	maximum(B7:D7)
8	Keenan	80	78	79	average(B8:D8)	maximum(B8:D8)
9						

In this example, the AVERAGE function is used in Column E to calculate the average mark obtained by each student. The AVERAGE function uses a range in the same way that the SUM function uses a range. You could, of course, input 'AVERAGE(B3,C3,D3)' but using a range is easier, especially if there are lots of cells involved. Again, the function only needs to be inserted once in to a cell—after this, you can copy it in to the remaining cells. Handy, isn't it!

The MAXIMUM values are shown in column F where, yet again, a range is used. The function 'MAXIMUM(B7:D7)' reads 'find the maximum value in the range B7 to D7'.

The MINIMUM values aren't shown. To find the minimum value, you would write something like 'MINIMUM(B3:D3)'. What would you write to find the minimum value for the range B4 to D4?

For You To Do

Find out how to use the average, maximum and minimum functions in the spreadsheet application you are using. Once you've done that, try the following exercise.

1. Create the spreadsheet shown above.
2. Insert the average and maximum functions in row 3 and copy these functions in to the other rows.
3. In a new column (G for example), insert a function to calculate the minimum test score and copy this function in to the other rows.
4. Enhance the spreadsheet as you see fit.
5. Save the completed spreadsheet as RESULTS and print out a copy of your work.

This spreadsheet lists the temperature (in degrees Celsius) in various world cities for the first week of July. Why are the temperatures in Perth and Johannesburg so low?

Assignment no. 60

For You To Do

	A	B	C	D	E	F
1	TEMPERATURE					
2		Dublin	Perth	Athens	Madrid	Johannesburg
3	01 July	23	16	35	32	19
4	02 July	24	16	36	33	20
5	03 July	22	15	35	30	18
6	04 July	20	17	34	31	19
7	05 July	21	15	35	36	21
8	06 July	19	16	36	34	18
9	07 July	19	14	37	35	19
10	Average					
11	Maximum					
12	Minimum					
13						

1. Create the spreadsheet shown above.
2. Insert a function to calculate the average temperature for Dublin.
3. Copy this function to each of the other cities.
4. Insert appropriate functions to calculate the maximum and minimum temperatures for Dublin.
5. Copy these functions to each of the other cities.
6. Carry out the following enhancements:
   - Make the city names bold;
   - Make the dates italic;
   - Change the font for the average, maximum and minimum titles.
7. Save the spreadsheet as CELSIUS and print out one copy.

Assignment no. 61 The data contained in this spreadsheet concerns eight of the planets in our solar system. Days are measured in Earth days (24 hrs), years are measured in Earth years (365 days), distance is measured in millions of kilometres, and size is measured relative to the size of the Earth (Earth is given a value of 1.0). Some of the values have been rounded off.

For You To Do

	A	B	C	D	E	F
1	PLANETS					
2		DAY	YEAR	DISTANCE (millions km)	SIZE	
3	MERCURY	59	0.25	58	0.06	
4	VENUS	243	0.6	108	0.8	
5	MARS	1	1.9	228	0.1	
6	JUPITER	0.5	12	778	318	
7	SATURN	0.5	29	1500	95	
8	URANUS	0.7	84	2875	14.50	
9	NEPTUNE	0.7	165	4500	17	
10	PLUTO	6.5	248	5900	0.004	
11						
12	Average					
13	Minimum					
	Maximum					

1. Create the spreadsheet using the data given.
2. Insert a function to find the average length of a day and copy this across each of the other statistics in the spreadsheet, i.e., year, distance and size.
3. Insert a function to calculate the minimum value for each set of statistics and copy this in to each column.
4. Insert a function to calculate the maximum value in a column and copy this in to each of the other columns.
5. Enhance the spreadsheet as you see fit.
6. Save the file as PLANET and print out a completed copy.

This is a simple spreadsheet which will calculate your budget needs. Note that the remainder from the first week becomes the opening balance of the second week. For example, if you have £5.00 left over from Week 1, then you will have £5.00 plus £200 (income) at the beginning of Week 2.

Assignment no. 62

For You To Do

	A	B	C	D	E	F	G
1	BUDGET						
2			WEEK 1	WEEK 2	WEEK 3	WEEK 4	TOTAL
3	Opening Balance		£0.00				
4	Income		£200	£200	£180	£210	
5	Total						
6	Expenses	rent	£50.00	£50.00	£50.00	£50.00	
7		food	£30.00	£38.00	£40.00	£42.00	
8		ESB	£10.00	£12.00	£10.00	£8.00	
9		heating	£12.00	£20.00	£15.00	£18.00	
10		cinema	£5.00	£0.00	£5.00	£5.00	
11		telephone	£8.00	£9.00	£8.00	£12.00	
12							
13	Total Expenses						
14	Remainder						

1. Create the spreadsheet using the data given and save as BUDGET.
2. In row 5, insert an appropriate function to add the opening balance and the income.
3. In row 13, insert a function to add together all the expenses for a week. Copy this to each of the other weeks.
4. In row 14, insert a formula to subtract the total expenses (row 13) from the total money available (row 5). Copy this to each of the other weeks.
5. In cell D3, insert the cell address for the remainder from Week 1 (C14).
6. In cell E3, the cell address will be the remainder for Week 2 (D14). Now complete F3 yourself.
7. In column G, insert a function to total each row.
8. Enhance the spreadsheet as you see fit.
9. Save your work again and print out one copy.

Absolute Cell Address

When you copy a formula from one cell address to another, you will have noticed that it changes automatically. Sometimes, however, you may not want the formula or cell address to change, you actually want it to remain the same. This is called an *absolute address*. Look at the following example.

Example

	A	B	C	D	E	F
1					VAT	21%
2	ITEM	COST	VAT	TOTAL		
3	Pentax Camera	£250	B3*F1	B3+C3		
4	Olympus Camera	£90	B4*F1	B4+C4		
5	Canon Camera	£150	B5*F1	B5+C5		
6						

In this spreadsheet, the cost of each camera is multiplied by the VAT rate, which is given in cell F1. A dollar sign before the column letter and another one before the row number denotes an absolute cell reference, e.g., F1. [**Note**: the spreadsheet package you are working with may denote an absolute cell reference slightly differently.]

Let's say you insert the first formula (B3*F1) in to cell C3. You then copy this formula to the other cells in the column. The first part of the formula will change (the B3 part), but the second part (F1) will not. This is because the second part is an absolute cell address.

What would happen if you didn't use an absolute cell address when you copied the formula to the other rows? You'd get an error message because the computer would change the second part of the formula. Cell D4 would contain B4*F2 (F2 contains nothing) and D5 would contain B5*F3 (and F3 contains nothing either).

In this particular example, the main advantage of using an absolute cell address is that you can see what would happen if VAT increased by one or two per cent. If you didn't use an absolute address, each cell formula would have to be changed individually.

For You To Do

1. Create the spreadsheet shown above and find out how to use the absolute address function in your spreadsheet application.
2. Insert the appropriate formula in C3 which contains an absolute address. Copy this formula to the other cells in Column C. Does the absolute address change?
3. Then insert the formula again without using an absolute address. Copy this formula to the other cells. Did you get an error message? Why?

In this assignment, you will use an absolute cell address. The spreadsheet shown below is used in a hotel to calculate each customer's total bill.

Assignment no. 63

	A	B	C	D	E	F	G
1				VAT	21%		
2							
3	Customer	Price/Night	No. of Nights	Room Service	Subtotal	Tax	TOTAL
4	Adams	£20	7	£15.00			
5	Barlow	£20	1	£0.00			
6	Smith	£30	2	£0.00			
7	O'Brien	£20	7	£10.00			
8	O'Neill	£30	14	£37.50			
9	Carroll	£20	7	£24.50			
10	Williams	£35	3	£12.00			
11	Butler	£25	1	£0.00			
12	Firth	£35	7	£23.60			
13	Owens	£35	14	£28.89			

1. Create the spreadsheet shown above.
2. Insert an appropriate formula in E4 to work out the Subtotal. (Hint: Multiply the cost per night by the number of nights and add room service.)
3. Copy this formula to the other rows.
4. Using an absolute address, insert a formula under Tax to calculate the amount of VAT payable per customer. (Hint: It will probably be something like E4*E1.)
5. Copy this formula to the other rows.
6. Insert a formula to calculate the TOTAL and copy this to the other rows.
7. Change E1 to 23%. How does this affect the spreadsheet?
8. Enhance the spreadsheet as you see fit.
9. Save the spreadsheet as HOTEL and print out one copy.

Assignment no. 64 Here's another spreadsheet which makes use of an absolute cell address. In this example, a shopkeeper is giving a discount of 10% on all his stock and wishes to work out new prices for the goods on sale.

For You To Do

	A	B	C	D	E
1				DISCOUNT	10%
2					
3	ITEM	OLD_PRICE	DISCOUNT	NEW_PRICE	SAVING
4	OLYMPUS 120	120			
5	ZOOM LENS	80			
6	PENTAX 400	130			
7	CANON XZ12	290			
8	COLOUR FILTER	30			
9	LUNAR SPORT	45			
10	JAVA GOLD	59			
11	OLYMPUS ZOOM	90			
12	KODAK FUN	10			
13	KELPLER ZODIAC	130			

1. Create the spreadsheet shown above.
2. In cell C4, insert a formula using an absolute cell address to work out the discount. Copy this to all the other rows.
3. In cell D4, insert a formula to calculate the new price. Copy this formula to all the other rows.
4. In cell E4, insert a formula to calculate the saving made on this item. Copy this formula to each of the other rows.
5. Format the cells from B4 to E13 as currency to two decimal places.
6. Enhance the spreadsheet as you see fit.
7. Change the discount in cell E1 from 10% to 15%.
8. Save the spreadsheet as SALE and print out one copy.

This spreadsheet uses two absolute cell addresses. One is used to add VAT and another to include a fixed profit margin. See how you get on!

Assignment no. 65

For You To Do

	A	B	C	D	E
1			VAT=	21%	
2			MARGIN=	16%	
3	ITEM	WHOLESALE PRICE	MARGIN	VAT	RETAIL
4					
5	Pillowcase	£3.40			
6	Single Sheet (cotton)	£4.68			
7	Single Sheet (nylon)	£4.89			
8	Double Sheet (nylon)	£6.78			
9	Single Duvet (down)	£23.78			
10	Single Duvet (polyester)	£13.67			
11	Double Duvet	£24.00			
12	King-size Duvet	£35.68			
13	Curtains (muslin)	£12.78			

1. Create the spreadsheet shown above.
2. In cell C5, insert a formula using an absolute cell address to calculate the Profit Margin on this item. Copy this to all the other rows.
3. In cell D5, insert a formula using an absolute cell address to calculate the VAT on this item. Copy this formula to all the other rows.
4. In cell E5, insert a formula to calculate the Retail Price of the item. Copy this formula to all the other rows.
5. Format the cells from B5 to E13 as currency to two decimal places.
6. Enhance the spreadsheet as you see fit.
7. Change the profit margin value in cell D2 from 16% to 12%.
8. Save this spreadsheet as PROFIT and print out one copy.

Adding/Deleting Rows and Columns

Sometimes it is necessary to add or delete rows or columns. This can enhance the look of a spreadsheet. Look at the two examples below—which do you find easier to read?

Example A

	A	B	C	D	E	F
1	EXECUTIVE	WEEK 1	WEEK 2	WEEK 3	WEEK 4	TOTAL
2	Johnson	1220	900	980	1100	
3	Friel	1500	1260	1700	1900	
4	Murphy	1300	1250	1350	1400	
5	Total					

Example B

	A	B	C	D	E	F	G
1							
2	EXECUTIVE	WEEK 1	WEEK 2	WEEK 3	WEEK 4		TOTAL
3							
4	Johnson	1220	900	980	1100		
5	Friel	1500	1260	1700	1900		
6	Murphy	1300	1250	1350	1400		
7							
8	Total						

Clearly, Example B is easier to read. The figures aren't heaped on top of each other as in Example A. The layout in B was achieved by simply adding empty rows and columns to separate groups of data from each other. The result is a clear and easy-to-follow spreadsheet.

If you wish to insert a row or column, and you have already entered formulae into the spreadsheet, there is no need to re-enter the formulae again as the computer will automatically update all your formulae for you. Remember, a spreadsheet can be huge, so don't be miserly about space!

For You To Do

1. Find out how to insert/delete rows and columns in your spreadsheet application.
2. Create the spreadsheet shown in Example A above and insert the appropriate formulae.
3. Insert the additional rows and columns shown in Example B. Note how the formulae change automatically.

This assignment requires you to insert and delete columns after you've created the spreadsheet and input formulae.

Assignment no. 66

	A	B	C	D	E	F
1	EXAM RESULTS	Exam 1	Exam 2	Exam 3	Exam 4	AVERAGE
2	J. Smith	56	60	65	70	
3	P. Hogan	45	49	55	58	
4	J. Lewis	57	58	52	50	
5	S. Conway	40	45	48	42	
6	D. Evans	70	75	65	70	
7	P. Heuston	86	82	88	90	
8	B. Dylan	94	90	89	93	
9	C. Molloy	30	35	30	39	
10	G. McGraw	59	56	58	57	
11	M. Carey	64	62	66	64	
12	Average					
13						

1. Create the spreadsheet shown above.
2. Insert the appropriate formulae in cells F2 and B12 to calculate the average mark for each student and for each exam.
3. Copy these formulae to the other rows and columns.
4. Insert a row between row 1 and row 2.
5. Insert a column between A and B and another between E and F.
6. Insert a row after the last student (M. Carey) and before the Average row.
7. Enhance the spreadsheet as follows:
   - Make the headings in row 1 bold and right justified;
   - Put column A in italics.
8. Save the spreadsheet as EXAM and print out one copy.

Written Test

These questions are designed to test your understanding of everything that has been explained so far about spreadsheets. Good luck!

1. What is meant by 'cell address'?

2. In Spreadsheet A, what is the address of the cell that contains the value '1492'?

3. What value is contained in cell B2?

4. What formula would you use in cell E3 to calculate the total for Region A?

Spreadsheet A

	A	B	C	D	E
1					
2	Region	Jones	Smith	Adams	Total
3	A		1200	1250	1260
4	B		1300	1278	1678
5	C		1400	1345	1492
6	Total				

5. What formula would you use in cell B6 to calculate Jones' total?

6. What is meant by a 'range' of cells?

7. When working with a spreadsheet, why do we use cell addresses and not the values contained in them?

8. In Spreadsheet A, how would you find the average of the values in each Region?

9. What is meant by 'absolute cell address'?

10. Explain the difference between copying a formula that uses an absolute cell address and one that doesn't?

11. In Spreadsheet B, which cell would you refer to using an absolute address?

12. What formula would you use to calculate the VAT on shampoo?

13. What formula would you use to find the retail price of toothpaste?

Spreadsheet B

	A	B	C	D
1			VAT	21%
2	ITEM	Cost	VAT	Retail
3	Shampoo	1.89		
4	Toothpaste	1.50		
5	Soap	0.45		

14. Name any two ways you could enhance Spreadsheet B.

15. Explain how you would format cells B3 to D5 as currency values to two decimal places.

Charts and Graphs

The graph and chart function in a spreadsheet is one of the easiest features to use. As the saying goes, 'a picture is worth a thousand words'. Graphs and charts help make complex series of numbers understandable and it is well worth your while learning how to use this feature.

Example

The spreadsheet in this example shows the prices of various company shares, which are listed on the stock market, over a five-month period. Compare the spreadsheet with the chart underneath which shows the same information in a visual form!

	A	B	C	D	E	F
1	SHARES	12-Mar	12-Apr	12-May	12-Jun	12-Jul
2						
3	GOLDEN VALE	79	70	60	68	70
4	SMURFIT	225	200	180	200	235
5	TULLOW OIL	110	80	73	110	115
6						

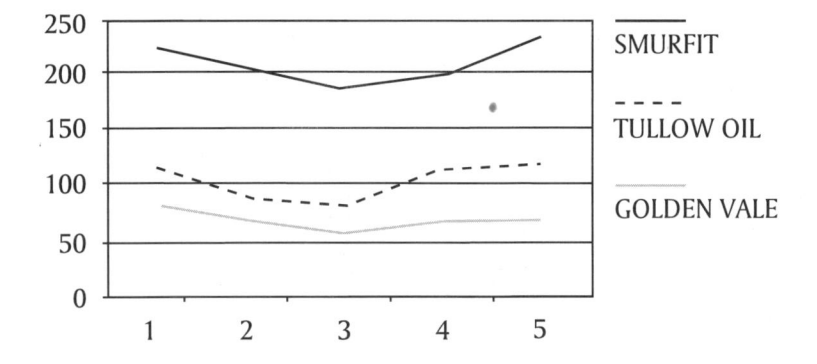

There are many different types of graphs and charts that can be used with a spreadsheet. Whatever one you choose to use should enhance the presentation of the data and not detract from it. For example, if a pie chart had been used in the example above, it would have been of limited value as it wouldn't have conveyed the information as clearly as the line graph does.

Find out how to convert a spreadsheet to a graph in your spreadsheet application. Use the share data given above as practice material until you are familiar with the process.

Assignment no. 67 This spreadsheet contains data which is best displayed in a graph or chart. It refers to the sales figures for a garage over a four-month period. (The graph is made up of different patterns in black/white.)

For You To Do

	A	B	C	D
1	JOHNSON CAR SALES			
2				
3		MAY	JUNE	JULY
4	MONDEO	4	7	3
5	ESCORT	5	8	10
6	FIESTA	2	3	2
7	CORSA	6	9	12
8	VECTRA	6	7	3
9	VW GOLF	10	12	15
10	VW JETTA	13	11	12
11	CARINA	15	16	13
12	COROLLA	16	14	15
13				

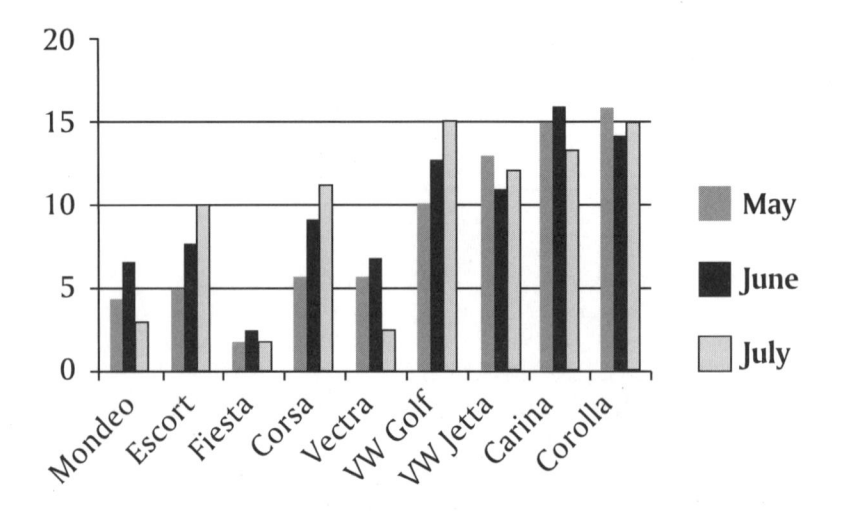

See if you can reproduce the spreadsheet and chart as shown above. Black and white patterns should be used if you are printing on a black and white printer. If you're fortunate enough to have a colour printer, you can use colour in the bars of your chart.

The spreadsheet below contains a list of European countries and the amount of glass each collects for recycling (in tonnes). It also gives the percentage that this figure represents of total national consumption. (This list was compiled in 1988—things have improved enormously since then.)

Assignment no. 68

	A	B	C	D
1				
2	Country	Tonnes	%	
3	Austria	115,000	54	
4	Belgium	208,000	60	
5	Denmark	58,000	36	
6	Finland	18,000	36	
7	France	760,000	38	
8	W. Germany	1,538,000	53	
9	Britain	310,000	17	
10	Greece	14,000	13	
11	Ireland	11,000	13	
12	Italy	670,000	42	
13	Netherlands	279,000	57	
14	Norway	11,000	24	
15	Portugal	34,000	14	
16	Spain	287,000	24	
17	Sweden	42,000	34	
18	Switzerland	164,000	56	

1. Create the spreadsheet shown above.
2. Enhance the spreadsheet as you see fit.
3. Create a bar chart showing the relationship between each country.
4. Save your work as RECYCLE and print out a copy of both the spreadsheet and the chart.

Assignment no. 69 A friend asks you to input share price information, which she has been collecting over a three-week period, in to a spreadsheet. She wants to know which shares, if any, are steadily climbing and which ones are falling in price. Construct the spreadsheet as shown below and then follow the instructions given.

For You To Do

	A	B	C	D	E	F
1	SHARE PRICES					
2		AIB	BOI	CRH	KERRY GROUP	HIBERNIAN
3	1/01	618	846	729	667	410
4	2/01	615	840	724	670	413
5	3/01	615	835	721	775	417
6	4/01	612	832	715	678	418
7	5/01	612	830	716	680	420
8	8/01	610	825	712	675	426
9	9/01	608	826	710	673	429
10	10/01	609	828	707	670	433
11	11/01	605	830	702	670	435
12	12/01	602	834	700	665	440
13	14/01	599	838	698	662	443
14	15/01	595	843	698	661	440
15	16/01	590	850	699	600	438
16	17/01	593	855	700	598	435
17	18/01	589	858	702	595	430
18						

1. Once you've created the spreadsheet, insert a new row between rows 2 and 3 and add a new column between columns A and B.
2. Enhance the spreadsheet as you see fit.
3. Create a chart showing the trend of share prices against time.
4. Save this spreadsheet as SHARE and print out a copy of both the spreadsheet and the chart.

The following spreadsheet will help you work out how much money you need to save each month in order to have £1,000 in three years time. Compound interest is calculated by multiplying the principal (the amount of money) plus the interest from previous years, by the interest rate, and then dividing by 100. For example, if you had £100 in a bank for 3 years, earning interest at 4%, your calculations would be as follows:

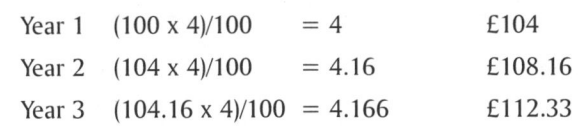

Assignment no. 70

For You To Do

Year 1   (100 x 4)/100   = 4   £104
Year 2   (104 x 4)/100   = 4.16   £108.16
Year 3   (104.16 x 4)/100   = 4.166   £112.33

In the spreadsheet below, interest is calculated at the end of each year.

	A	B	C	D	E
1		Interest Rate	4.5%		
2					
3	Savings per month	Year	Principal	Interest	Total
4	£10	1	A4*12	(C4*C1)	C4+D4
5	£20	2	(A5*12)+E4		
6	£25	3			
7					

1. Create the spreadsheet shown above.
2. The formulae you need to use are given in cells C4, C5 and D4. In Year 1, the principal (C4) is determined by multiplying the amount saved each month by 12. The interest (D4) is calculated by multiplying the principal by the interest rate (C1). Note that this formula uses an absolute cell address.
3. In Year 2, the same calculations are carried out. However, the total for Year 1 (E4, principal plus interest) should first be added to the principal for Year 2.
4. Copy the formula in D4 to D5 and the formula in E4 to E5.
5. Fill in the formulae required for Year 3 (copy from the previous row).
6. You can now change the amount saved each month in order to find out how much you need to save to have £1,000 by the end of Year 3. Try also changing the interest rate in C1 to see how it affects the total.
7. Save this spreadsheet as COMPOUND and print out one copy.

Assignment no. 71
Part 1

In this assignment you are required to create a spreadsheet showing a profit and loss account for a trading company.

	A	B	C	D	E
1	ACME TRADING 1998				
2					
3	SALES			40,000	
4	LESS RETURNS			4,000	
5	NET SALES				
6					
7	OPENING STOCK		10,000		
8	PURCHASES	20,000			
9	LESS RETURNS	5,000			
10					
11					
12	CARRIAGE INWARDS		400		
13	DUTY ON GOODS		800		
14					
15	LESS CLOSING STOCK		2,200		
16	GROSS PROFIT				

1. Create the spreadsheet shown above.
2. In cell D5, insert a formula to calculate the Net Sales (Sales less Returns).
3. In cell C9, insert a formula that subtracts Returns from Purchases.
4. In cell C10, insert a formula that adds the Opening Stock to the value in C9.
5. In cell C14, insert a formula that adds the value in C10 plus Carriage Inwards plus Duty On Goods.
6. In cell D15, insert a formula that subtracts Less Closing Stock from the value in C14.
7. To calculate the Gross Profit, insert a formula in D16 that subtracts D15 from D5.
8. Save this spreadsheet as PROFIT.

Retrieve the file PROFIT and add the following data to the spreadsheet.

Assignment no. 71
Part 2

	A	B	C	D	E
17	LESS EXPENSES				
18	TELEPHONE		600		
19	ESB		1,200		
20	STATIONERY		200		
21	COMMISSION		500		
22	ADVERTISING		1,500		
23	BAD DEBTS		550		
24					
25	NET PROFIT				
26					

1. In cell D23, insert a formula to calculate the Total Expenses.
2. In cell D25, insert a formula to subtract the Total Expenses from the Gross Profit (D16).
3. Enhance the spreadsheet as follows:
   - Make the text in column A bold;
   - Put the text in column B in italics;
   - Make the data in column D bold.
4. Save these changes to your file and print out one copy of the completed spreadsheet.

Using 'IF'

Consider the following scenario: an employer wants the spreadsheet application on his computer to automatically calculate if employees qualify for an end-of-year bonus. Employees only qualify for this bonus if they have sold more than £12,000 worth of goods during the year. If they do not meet this target, they miss out on the bonus. The spreadsheet calculates the amount of sales during the year as follows:

	A	B	C	D	E
1		Jones	Smith	Keenan	
2	Jan	800	860	900	
3	Feb	700	750	800	
4	Mar	800	890	920	
5	Apr	600	900	950	
6	May	900	980	1000	
7	June	1200	1300	760	
8	July	1300	1200	1100	
9	Aug	1100	1150	1170	
10	Sep	1150	1170	1090	
11	Oct	1000	800	950	
12	Nov	950	900	1130	
13	Dec	980	1300	1100	
14	Total				

In cell B14, the employer enters a formula—SUM(B2:B13)—to add up the total sales for Jones during the year. This formula is then copied to the other columns. A formula must then be inserted which will determine whether a salesperson qualifies for a bonus of £100. This is entered in B15 and reads as follows:

IF(B14>12000,100,0)

In other words, if the data in B14 (the amount sold by Jones during the year) is greater than 12,000, then write 100, otherwise write 0. This is known as the *logical if* function. It is generally written as

IF(CONDITION,TRUE,FALSE)

Check your own spreadsheet application and find out how this function is written.

Try answering the following questions which use the 'IF' function.

Assignment no. 72

1. A sales executive will get a bonus of £200 if she sells more than £1,000 worth of goods in a month. Cell D4 contains the data for the amount sold last month. Which of the following is the correct formula to use?

a) IF(D4>1000,200,0) b) IF(D4<1000,200,0)
c) IF(D4>1000,0,200) d) IF(D4<1000,200,200)

2. If a student gets over 50 marks in an exam, he will pass. Which of the following formulae would you use if the exam mark information is contained in cell F5?

a) IF(F5>50,'FAIL','PASS') b) IF(F5<50,'PASS','FAIL')
c) IF(F5>50,'PASS','FAIL') d) IF(F5<50,'PASS','PASS')

3. An airline charges an excess baggage fee of £15 if the weight of a suitcase is over 20 kg. The cell address of the weight data is D15. Which of the following formulae is correct?

a) IF(D15>20,15,0) b) IF(D15>20,0,15)
c) IF(D15<20,15,0) d) IF(D15>20,15,15)

4. A student will get an A grade this term if his average mark, over a series of tests, is greater than or equal to 85. His average mark information is contained in cell G4. Which of the following is the correct formula to use?

a) IF(G4>85,'Grade A',0) b) IF(G4>=85,'Grade A',0)
c) IF(G4>85,0,'Grade A') d) IF(G4>=85,0,'Grade A')

5. Write out the formula required to calculate whether commission is due on the number of car sales in January. Commission is only due if more than 15 cars are sold. The number of cars sold is given in cell A12. If commission is due, write 'DUE', otherwise nothing.

6. Write out the formula you would use to work out whether the average test mark is greater than or equal to 50. The mark is contained in cell C9. If it is greater than or equal to 50, write 'greater', otherwise write 'less'.

7. Write a formula that calculates whether the data in F9 is less than or equal to 10. If the condition is true, write 'TRUE' and if it's false, write 'FALSE'.

Assignment no. 73 The following spreadsheet keeps a record of students' exam results over the course of a term. The average mark for each student is determined and the spreadsheet then checks this average mark against the pass mark. If their average mark is greater than or equal to the pass mark, the spreadsheet writes 'PASS' beside the student's name, otherwise the student fails.

	A	B	C	D	E
1		EXAM 1	EXAM 2	EXAM 3	AVERAGE
2	JONES	45	50	55	
3	SMITH	55	57	59	
4	PETERSON	58	62	65	
5	MITCHELL	67	65	63	
6	FRIEL	56	60	59	
7	O'CONNELL	30	35	38	
8	MCGOVERN	70	72	73	
9	HARTE	69	70	75	
10	JOHNSON	79	80	82	
11	MOONEY	71	75	79	
12	FITZGERALD	45	49	54	
13					
14	PASS MARK	55			

1. Create the spreadsheet shown above.
2. In cell E2, insert a formula to calculate the average mark. Copy this formula in to each of the other rows.
3. In cell F1, insert 'PASS/FAIL'.
4. In cell F2, insert a formula to determine whether the student has passed or failed. The formula will look something like IF(E2>=B14,'PASS','FAIL'). Note that the cell containing the pass mark (B14) is referred to by an absolute address. Copy this formula to the other rows.
5. Change the pass mark in cell B14 to 60. How many students failed?
6. Save this spreadsheet as MARKS and print out one copy.

A garage gives commission to each sales executive at the end of every month. A sales executive will only get commission if they have sold more than a certain number of cars. The commission is calculated as a percentage of the total sales.

Assignment no.

For You To Do

	A	B	C	D	E	F	G
1	Executive	Week 1	Week 2	Week 3	Week 4	TOTAL	QUALIFY
2							
3	O'BRIEN	3	2	3	5		
4	O'HARA	3	3	3	5		
5	MURPHY	3	4	3	3		
6	HOLMES	3	2	0	1		
7	WALSHE	2	1	5	4		
8	MCKENNA	1	2	5	3		
9	KENNY	4	4	3	4		
10	BYRNE	2	3	4	5		
11	COURTNEY	2	4	3	3		
12	ROONEY	1	3	2	5		
13	Sales Needed	13					
14	Commission	25%					

1. Create the spreadsheet shown above.
2. In cell F3, insert a formula to calculate O'Brien's sales total over the four weeks. Copy this to the other rows.
3. In cell G3, insert a formula to determine whether each executive qualifies for commission. An executive will qualify if their total sales are greater than or equal to the value in B13. If they qualify, write 'Yes', otherwise write 'No'.
4. In column H, insert a formula to determine the amount of commission. The formula will be similar to this: IF(G3='YES',F3*B14,0). In other words, if the executive qualifies for commission, multiply their total sales by the value in B14. Copy this formula to the other rows and format the rows as currency.
5. Change the value in B13 to 10 and in B14 to 15%. What happens?
6. Save your work as COMM and print out one copy.

no. 75 A greengrocer wants a spreadsheet which will keep track of his stock and alert him when he needs to re-order a particular item. The spreadsheet below gives the wholesale price, the amount of boxes bought and the amount sold.

	A	B	C	D	E	F	G
1			VAT	21%			
2							
3	ITEM	WHOLESALE	VAT	RETAIL	BOUGHT	SOLD	REORDER
4	Cabbages	15			50	35	
5	Lettuce	20			45	29	
6	Carrots	11			20	15	
7	Mushrooms	80			15	12	
8	Turnips	20			40	30	
9	Parsnips	21			35	30	
10	Onions	22			10	8	
11	Tomatoes	42			20	14	
12	Beans	32			40	36	
13	Strawberries	80			35	29	
14							

1. Create the spreadsheet shown above.
2. In cell C4, insert a formula to calculate the VAT on each item by referring to the VAT rate in cell D1 (use an absolute address). Copy this formula to the other rows.
3. In cell D4, insert a formula to calculate the retail price. Copy this formula to the other rows.
4. In cell G4, insert a formula that uses the 'IF' function. The greengrocer only needs to reorder if he has sold more than 75% of his stock. If he has sold more than 75%, write 'REORDER', otherwise write 'OK'.
5. Enhance the spreadsheet as you see fit.
6. Save this spreadsheet as GROCER and print out one copy.

A livestock mart is using a spreadsheet to keep track of the animals sold. The spreadsheet lists the lot number, the number of animals, the buyer, the price and the commission due for each sale.

Assignment no. 7

	A	B	C	D	E
1					
2	LOT NO.	NUMBER	BUYER	PRICE	COMMISSION
3	101	3	NORRIS	1980	
4	102	2	MCBRIDE	1225	
5	103	5	ROBINSON	3211	
6	104	3	NORRIS	2480	
7	105	4	DOHERTY	3255	
8	106	2	HALPIN	1326	
9	107	3	BRADY	2455	
10	108	4	GORMAN	3310	
11	109	2	NORRIS	1288	
12	110	4	DEAN	3345	
13	111	3	NORRIS	1955	
14	112	4	GORMAN	3577	

1. Create the spreadsheet shown above.
2. Commission is based on the number of animals sold. The basic fee is £8.00 per animal. In cell E3, insert a formula to calculate the commission due on each lot.
3. Copy this formula to the other rows.
4. Animals sold to 'Norris' are going to the factory! In column F, insert a formula which will determine those lots that are going to the factory. Animals for the factory should have 'FACTORY' written beside them.
5. Enhance the spreadsheet as you see fit.
6. Format cells D3 to E14 as currency to two decimal places.
7. Save this spreadsheet as MART and print out one copy.

10. 77 A cruise ship has set up the spreadsheet shown below. The price of the cruise varies depending on the number of days travel. The basic price per day is £100. A passenger qualifies for a discount if they stay for more than eight days on the cruise.

	A	B	C	D	E	F
1	PASSENGER	NO. OF DAYS	PRICE	DISCOUNT	VAT	TOTAL
2	J. Jones	10				
3	K. Smith	8				
4	P. Johnson	8				
5	L. Lawlor	6				
6	P. Rooney	8				
7	T. Nelson	3				
8	R. Doyle	7				
9	R. Burke	7				
10	A. Sweeney	9				
11	A. Grier	14				
12	B. Kinsella	12				
13	VAT	21%				
14	Price/Day	£100				

1. Create the spreadsheet shown above.
2. In cell C2, insert a formula to calculate the cost of Jones' trip based on the data in B14.
3. Copy this formula to the other rows.
4. In cell D2, insert a formula to determine whether Jones' qualifies for a discount. In order to qualify, Jones must remain on board for at least eight days. If he qualifies, write '50', otherwise write nothing. Copy this to the other rows for the other passengers.
5. In cell E2, insert a formula to calculate the VAT on the cruise price (ignore the discount). Copy this to the other rows.
6. In cell F2, insert a formula to calculate the total price taking into account the discount. Copy this formula to the other rows.
7. Enhance the spreadsheet as follows:
   - Put column A in italics;
   - Make row 1 bold.
8. Format cells C2 to F14 as currency to two decimal places.
9. Burke has decided to stay on board for two more nights. Make this amendment.
10. Save the spreadsheet as CRUISE and print out one copy of your work.

Assessment Log Book

TASK	METHOD	DATE/SIGNATURE
Cell address	Oral, Written Test	
Formulae	Written Test, Assignment No. 53	
Saving and editing	Assignment Nos. 53, 55	
Enhancements	Assignment No. 54	
Sum and range	Assignment Nos. 56, 57	
Copying formulae (relative copying)	Assignment Nos. 58, 59	
Average, maximum and minimum	Assignment Nos. 60, 61	
Budget	Assignment No. 62	
Absolute cell address	Assignment Nos. 63, 64, 65	
Adding/deleting rows and columns	Assignment No. 66	
Charts and graphs	Assignment Nos. 67, 68, 69	
Compound interest	Assignment No. 70	
Profit and loss	Assignment No. 71	
Understanding 'IF'	Assignment No. 72	
Using 'IF'	Assignment Nos. 73–77	

COMBINED ASSIGNMENT

This assignment requires word processing, database and spreadsheet skills. It involves a camp site and there a four different elements to be carried out. It is not designed to be completed in one session so don't rush!

A camp site owner wants to create a leaflet (outlining the rules of the camp site), a questionnaire, a database (to hold the results of the questionnaire), and a spreadsheet (to calculate visitors' bills).

Part 1 Leaflet

LOCAL CAMPS
RULES

TIMETABLE

- Reception is open from 9.00 a.m. in the morning until 11.00 p.m. at night.
- Payment should be made before 1.00 p.m. on the day of departure. If payment is made after this time, you will be charged for another day.
- If you plan to leave before 9.00 a.m., payment can be made the previous evening.
- Silence should be observed from 11.00 p.m. until 8.00 a.m. for the convenience of other campers.
- Vehicles are not allowed in to the camp site after 8.00 p.m.

SITE

Camping pitches can only be assigned by reception staff. Pitches must not be changed without notifying reception. Please ensure that your ticket is displayed on your tent/caravan at all times. Any tents/caravans without a clearly displayed ticket will be removed from the site.

GAMES

Games are available in the restaurant. Please ensure that the games are returned as you found them.

SWIMMING POOL

Children under 10 years are allowed in the swimming pool only if accompanied by an adult.

Thank you for your co-operation.

Part 2
Questionnaire

LOCAL CAMPS

| 1 = poor |
| 2 = fair |
| 3 = average |
| 4 = good |
| 5 = excellent |

As part of our ongoing customer care programme, the management of Local Camps would appreciate your feedback. Please take the time to complete our questionnaire which will help us to improve our service. Please rate the following Local Camps facilities and services.

1. Cleanliness of the showers, toilets and washing areas
   1 2 3 4 5

2. Restaurant service and quality of food
   1 2 3 4 5

3. State of the grounds and sites
   1 2 3 4 5

4. Cleanliness and safety of swimming pool
   1 2 3 4 5

5. Personnel service
   Kitchen   1 2 3 4 5
   Restaurant   1 2 3 4 5
   Supermarket   1 2 3 4 5
   Reception   1 2 3 4 5
   Night Guard   1 2 3 4 5
   Cleaning Service   1 2 3 4 5

6. How did you hear of Local Camps?
   Camping Guide
   Tourist Office
   Friends
   Other

7. How many nights are you staying? _____

Thank you for taking the time to complete our questionnaire!

Part 3
Database

Eleven completed questionnaires have been returned to reception and the staff have input the results in to a database. Q1 refers to question 1 of the questionnaire, Q2 refers to question 2, etc. Question 5 has not been included. This is how the database looks:

NIGHTS	Q1	Q2	Q3	Q4	Q6
2	4	5	3	4	GUIDE
1	3	4	4	5	GUIDE
7	4	5	3	4	OFFICE
7	5	5	4	5	GUIDE
10	5	5	3	5	FRIEND
1	4	4	3	3	GUIDE
4	5	5	5	5	GUIDE
5	3	4	3	5	GUIDE
3	5	4	3	4	OFFICE
8	5	5	4	4	GUIDE
6	5	5	3	5	FRIEND

1. Create the database shown above paying attention to the name, width and datatype of each field.
2. Sort the database according to the NIGHTS field.
3. Search for respondents who stayed more than 7 nights.
4. Insert a formula that calculates the average rating for each question (except Q6).
5. What question received the lowest satisfaction rating?
6. How did most people hear about the camp site? (In other words, find out what was the most common response to Q6.)
7. Print the results of this search.
8. How many people rated the cleanliness and safety of the swimming pool at 3 or less?
9. Save your work as CAMP and print one copy of the complete database.

The management want to create a spreadsheet which will calculate the cost of each camper's stay. It will look something like this:

Part 4
Spreadsheet

	A	B	C	D	E
1			Cost/Night	TOTAL	
2	TENT		6		
3	CARAVAN		10		
4	CAR		2		
5	CAMPER VAN		14		
6	COST/PERSON		2		
7	VAT		21%		
8	TOTAL				
9					
10	No. of Nights		3		
11	No. of Persons		2		
12					

1. Create the spreadsheet shown above.
2. Insert a formula in cell D2 to calculate the cost based on the data in cell C10.
3. Copy this formula all the way down to cell D5.
4. In cell D6, insert a formula to calculate the cost based on the data in cell C11. (Multiply the total number of persons staying by the cost per person.)
5. Insert a formula in cell D7 to calculate VAT.
6. In cell D8, insert a formula to calculate the TOTAL.
7. Find out how much it would cost for two people with a car and caravan to stay for 5 nights.
8. Save this spreadsheet as COST and print out one copy.

PART V THE INTERNET

Introduction

What Is It? The Internet started in the 1960's when the U.S. Department of Defence set out to create a network of communication which was capable of withstanding a nuclear war. This process resulted in Internet Protocol (IP) technology being developed. Internet Protocol technology is the means by which all electronic messages are sent around the Internet.

In the 1980s, universities started to use the Internet—it was ideal for researchers doing collaborative work with other centres of education as it allowed regular and easy communication and information could be transferred in minutes rather than weeks. However, the system wasn't able to cope with the huge increase in traffic and, in 1987, the Internet that we know today was born. With this improved infrastructure, many smaller organisations started using the Internet. Today, the Internet is a highly dynamic environment—it changes constantly, with parts being updated, removed and added every minute of everyday.

Where Is It? The Net (an abbreviation for Internet) is everywhere. It consists of thousands of computers located all around the world that are joined together to form a huge network. No one single computer is responsible. There are hundreds of thousands of companies, universities and smaller networks all linked up together that share information and resources. Thus, the Net can't be said to be anywhere in particular—it's everywhere and any computer (with the necessary equipment) can link up to it!

Who Owns It? Nobody owns the Net and no one government controls it. The Net spans the jurisdictions of lots of countries. Many users are totally opposed to any government trying to control any part of the Net.

What Do I Need? In order to gain access to the Internet, the first things you need are a computer, a modem and a telephone line. Modem is short for MODulator DEModulator. It is a device that converts signals so that they can be transmitted over a telephone wire and then reconverts them when they arrive at the other end. Modems have different speeds (called baud rates) measured in bps (bauds per second). The faster the modem speed, the better.

Once you have a modem, a telephone line and a computer, you then need to connect to an ACCESS PROVIDER. This is a commercial company which sells access to the Internet. Usually you pay a once-off subscription fee and then a monthly rental fee. Different companies have different rates. The provider will send you software which directs the modem to dial the correct number. All you have to do is point and click! Apart from that, you must pay for the telephone call which connects you to your access provider each time you go online. Most calls are charged at local rates.

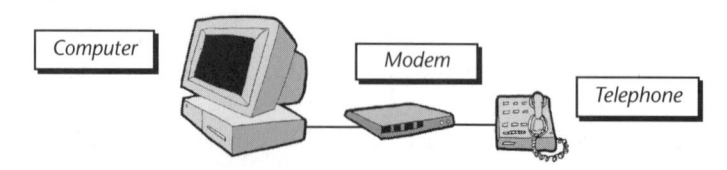

Parts of the Net

E-mail

The Internet is divided into different parts. The first part we'll look at is electronic mail, commonly known as e-mail. E-mail allows you to send data to anyone in the world with an e-mail address. You can even attach reports, spreadsheets, charts, etc. It is very fast (delivery can be made in seconds) and is virtually free. Many schools have e-mail addresses and this facilitates collaboration between them on various projects.

When using e-mail, don't type all your text in capitals as this is the electronic equivalent of shouting. Some people use signs in their e-mails to represent emotions. For example, if you want to indicate that you are happy, type :-) which is a smile, or to indicate sadness, type :-(which is an unhappy face. Internet users often refer to the normal method of mailing (i.e., the postman) as snail mail!

An e-mail address is made up of different parts. The first part is the person's identification—this can be a number or a name. The @ sign follows the identification and immediately after this, location information is given. For example, jsmith@iol.ie can be interpreted as the person jsmith at IOL (which is the name of the access provider, Ireland On-Line) in IE (which is a country abbreviation for Ireland). Here are some more examples:

djones@iol.ie

122233@indigo.ie

richardk@lcpdt.ac.uk

Newsgroups

Newsgroups are concerned with 'discussing' various topics, ranging from astronomy to pet health care! Each one focuses on a particular theme. Essentially, you submit your message to the newsgroup and it can be seen by anyone who joins the group. Many newsgroups require you to register before you are allowed to join in the 'discussion'.

When you look up the different newsgroups available on the Internet, you will find there are thousands of them!

Newsgroup names *usually* give an indication of the subject matter discussed. For example, something with the name 'astron.sci' is probably a newsgroup related to astronomy. There is no way of knowing for sure though, unless you join up!

Newsgroups are useful as a source of information if you have a particular query. For instance, if you have a problem with your computer, you could join a newsgroup which discusses computer problems, post your message and see what people have to say.

IRC

IRC stands for Internet Relay Chat. With IRC, you join a chat session and post your comments/views. The other chat participants then respond to what you've said immediately. It is just like 'talking' with people in real time. IRC differs from e-mail and newsgroups in that you must join in the discussion as it is happening. E-mail will hold your messages until you read them, IRC won't.

The Web The World Wide Web (or the Web as it is often called) is the part of the Internet that most people will have heard about or seen. This is because it is so easy to use. Accessing the Web requires a 'browser' application with a GUI (a graphical user interface) and it is this GUI which makes the Web so easy to navigate. All you have to do is point and click! Linking to the Web is easy, your access provider will send you the necessary software.

On the Web, you will come across pictures, sounds and animations. Each screen you access is called a 'page'. Within a page, you can click on highlighted words which will take you to another topic or page. These are called hyperlinks.

You can visit Web sites located all over the world. There are pictures of the moons of Jupiter, old masters in the Louvre, clip art and sounds that you can use, virtual libraries, historical documents, in fact nearly everything imaginable is out there waiting for you!

Search Engines Because of the vast amount of information on the Web, it is important that you navigate it efficiently. Otherwise you can waste a lot of time. Luckily, search engines have made this process manageable. A search engine is a program that goes and searches the Web for whatever keyword you've input. For example, if you wanted to go to the FBI Web site (maybe to check if you're on the Wanted Persons list!), you would type 'FBI' in to the search engine query box, and the search engine would then trawl the Web for relevant sites. It will list the results of its search as a set of hyperlinks on a separate page. The more information you give the search engine, the better chance it will have of finding what you're looking for.

If you know the address of the site you want to visit, just type the address in to your browser address box to go directly to it. One example of a Web site address is http://www.city.net/ which offers information on cities all over the world. Another is http://www.kpix.com/live/ which shows live pictures of San Francisco. This site is updated every 20 minutes.

It is possible to 'bookmark' a particular site if you plan to visit it regularly. This saves you from having to remember the address and type it in each time. Very useful once you become a frequent surfer.

Home Page A home page is the 'front door' page of a Web site. Web sites can be any size—they can consist of a single home page or, as is the case with more elaborate sites, they can contain a home page which has many other pages linked to it. A home page is simple to create (more about that later).

As with most things, some sites are great, while others are not so great. A site can contain text, sound and pictures. Do remember though, the more graphics a Web page contains, the longer it takes to download that page (and the more expensive your phone charges will be as a result!). It is for this reason that you can turn off graphics in your browser as this helps the site download faster.

Surfing the Web can present a few problems. One of these is junk mail. Some programmes can detect your e-mail address when you visit a site, and you could then find yourself bombarded with junk e-mail. While this is annoying, it is not as unpleasant as your computer picking up a virus while browsing the Web. Some nasty people can create what appears to be a lovely site, with perhaps a fun game to entice you to visit. Once you hit the site, the virus downloads on to your computer. Be careful where you visit!

Creating a Site

Creating your own Web site is well within your reach as there is lots of software available to help you. You don't even need to know HTML (the programming language which Web pages are written in). You should bear in mind the following few points before embarking on your own site.

1. Don't overload each page with information. If there is too much text on a page, people won't bother reading it. It is more difficult to read text on a computer screen than on paper, so keep to the point and be concise.
2. Keep sentences clear and uncluttered.
3. Use graphics and pictures sparingly—don't overdo it. Too many graphics on a page will result in the page taking longer to download.
4. Insert hyperlinks to other pages within your site, as well as to other interesting sites.
5. Check out other home pages for ideas on how to structure your own. Several schools have created excellent home pages demonstrating great design skill.
6. Include your e-mail address on your site if you have one.
7. Make sure your site is easy to navigate. Consider using both text hyperlinks and graphic/icon hyperlinks.

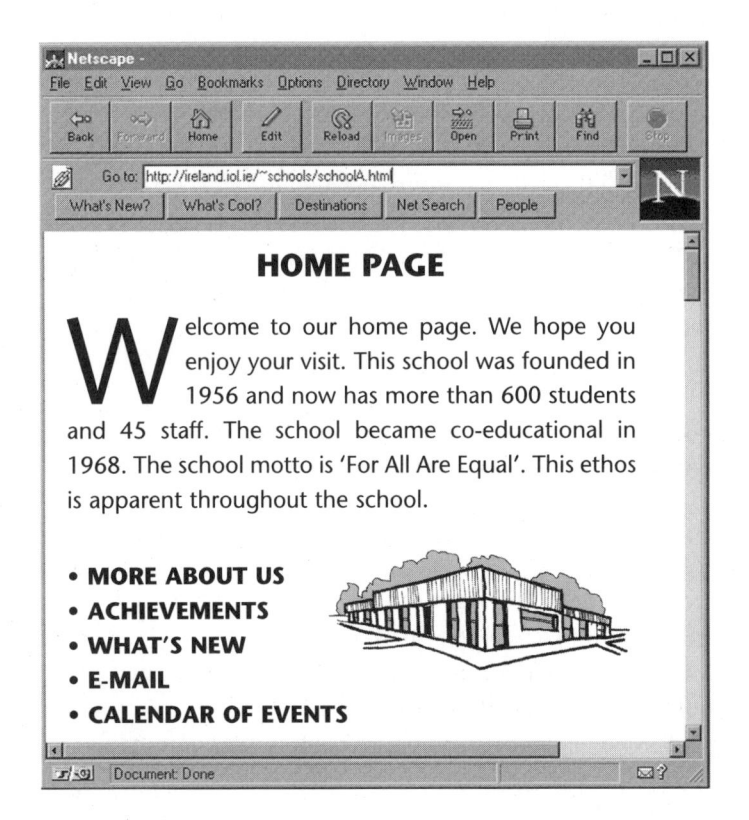

Example

The following two pages list educational Web sites which you may be interested in. The prefix HTTP:// should be inserted before all of these. Web addresses change all the time so some of these may be obsolete by the time you visit them!

German
www.goethe.de/ (Goethe Institute Munich)
www.goethe.de/gr/dub/enindex.htm (Goethe Institute Dublin)
www.goethe.de/z/demindex.htm (German teaching materials)
netguide.de/A/AA/aa1.htm (Net guide to German sites)
www.texhaus.com (Online German language learning)
library.byu.edu/~rdh/eurodocs/ (German documents)
www.welt.de/ (Die Welt)
194.163.254.145/aktuell/aktuell.html (Der Speigel)

French
www.francenet.fr/franceweb/FWCarnetRoute.html (French Web sites)
ccat.sas.upenn.edu/romance/Basic/fren.html (Complete French course)
www.minitel.fr (Minitel)
library.byu.edu/~rdh/euro/french.html (French documents)
www.lemonde.fr (Le Monde)
www.liberation.fr (Liberation)

History
www.hyperhistory.com (World history chart)
www.historychannel.com
www.thehistorynet.com
www.historyplace.com
history.rutgers.edu/oralhistory/orlhom.htm (Oral history archives of WWII)
www.nsstate.edu/Archives/History/USA/WWII/ww2.html (WWII archives)

Geography
www.intergo.com/library/ref/atlas/atlas.htm (World atlas)
www.nationalgeographic.com/resources/ngo/maps (View maps of the world)
www.odci.gov (World factbook)

Art
sunsite.unc.edu (Louvre)
www.arthouse.ie (Arthouse multimedia centre in Dublin)
www.arts.ufl.edu (College of Fine Arts)

E-Pals
www.stolaf.edu/network/iecc (E-mail pals, learn a language with a native speaker)

Science
www.dunsink.dias.ie/ (Dunsink Observatory)
spacelink.nasa.gov/index.html (NASA and library especially for education)
pages.prodigy.com/IASTE/iaste2.htm (Science museum)
mwanal.lanl.gov/CST/imagemap/periodic/periodic.html (Periodic table of elements)
www.si.edu (Smithsonian Institute)

www.lib.uconn.edu (Artic Circle)
www.drscience.com (Dr Science answers questions!)
www.dinosauria.com (Dinosaurs)
www.discovery.com (Web counterpart of TV channel)
www.exploratorium.edu (Dozens of interactive experiments)
www.fi.edu (Franklin Institute Science Museum)
www.lib.washington.edu (Links to natural history museums and collections)

Literature

the-tech.mit.edu/Shakespeare/ (Complete works of Shakespeare)
www.leeds.ac.uk/theatre/emd/links.htm (Medieval drama links)
www.lib.ncsu.edu (ALEX, electronic texts)
classics.mit.edu (400 Greek/Roman texts in English)

Business

www.amex.com (American Stock Exchange)
www.economist.com (The Economist)
kola.dcu.ie/~bstai (Business Studies Teachers Association of Ireland)
ireland.iol.ie (IBEC)
www.itw.ie (Irish Trade Web)
bized.ac.uk (BizEd)
www.info.ft.com (Financial Times)

Sites You Must See!

kola.dcu.ie/~iednet/index.htm (Irish Education Web—schools, projects, links, subjects, etc. A must for teachers and students alike.)
ericir.sunsite.syr.edu/ (Educational Resources Information Centre)
www.bbc.co.uk/education/
www.educationindex.com (Excellent index of links to educational sites)
www.infoshare.ca/csm/index.htm (Cyber magazine for schools)
george.lbl.gov/ITG.hm.pg.docs/dissect/info.html (This site shows the dissection of a frog from various angles. Well worth a visit.)
www.specialoperations.com/intelligence.html (CIA, FBI, etc.!)

These sites are only a small selection of all the sites on the Web. They should, however, provide you with a good starting point from which to commence surfing!